# DICTIONARY OF CONTEMPORARY THOUGHT

## David Kirby

# M

**MACMILLAN PRESS**
LONDON

Macmillan Reference Books

First published in 1984 by
THE MACMILLAN PRESS LTD
London and Basingstoke
Associated Companies throughout the world

ISBN 0 333 36980 7 hard cover
ISBN 0 333 37270 0 paperback

British Library Cataloguing in Publication Data
Kirby, David
    A dictionary of contemporary thought.
    1. Encyclopedias and dictionaries
    I. Title
    032  AE5

ISBN 0-333-36980-7
ISBN 0-333-3727-0 Pbk

Printed and bound in Hong Kong

For A. C. K.

"To punish me for my contempt for authority,
Fate made me an authority myself."

The eternal mystery of the world is its intelligibility.

*Albert Einstein*


Why is there anything at all rather than nothing?

*Leibniz*

# CONTENTS

# PREFACE

A recent newspaper column begins: "The one thing that students most need as they enter college, and the one thing they are least likely to get, is a greater emphasis on interdisciplinary studies. They need to learn how one subject relates to another, how one discipline affects or modifies the influence of another—in short, how things hang together in a totality."

What is called for here is an understanding of something that might be described as the plural world, an OXYMORON that suggests that there is but a single world, yet one that is seen and described plurally (all terms used in this preface and defined in the text will be capitalized). The scientists have their languages, the philosophers theirs, and so on. There are even languages within languages: there is no BIG-BANG THEORY but a number of big-bang theories, for example, no EXISTENTIALISM but a variety of existentialisms. At the same time that knowledge is increasingly compartmentalized, however, the walls that separate one compartment from the next are increasingly broken down by the growing universality of education, the increasing ease and low cost of the spread of information, and sheer curiosity about what other people are doing and thinking. As a result, even the most diehard specialists are finding it not only convenient but also necessary to borrow from the languages of disciplines other than their own.

Too, if this world is plural, each of its seers, these aforementioned specialists, is plural as well—it is hard to attend a colloquium or pick up a scholarly journal these days without coming across a phrase like "we are all existentialists," "we are all REALISTS," "we are all NEW CRITICS," and so on. If these statements are true (or false and deserving of refutation), then it would behoove us to know who we are. Hence this book, which appropriates key terms from the principal languages of the mind, defines them, and demonstrates their interdisciplinary applicability.

The main emphasis in this glossary is on learning not through biographical studies or analogy but through the languages themselves. Anyone with fluency in a foreign tongue knows that translation, while superior to total inaccessibility, is inferior to the understanding of the text that comes with a knowledge of its original language. Words are tools; to many they are the most useful tools, while to others they are the only tools available, and as mathematician Morris Kline says, "Intellectually oriented people must be fully aware of the powers of the tools at their disposal." This glossary is intended as a start, a collection of the basic tools necessary for intellectual labor.

I first felt the need for a basic interdisciplinary vocabulary some years ago. As a literary person, I found myself referring occasionally to ABSTRACT EXPRESSIONISM or the UNCERTAINTY PRINCIPLE or ZENO'S PARADOXES and wondering if I were being as correct as I wanted to be. Discussing the problem with colleagues, I began to encounter scientists and social scientists who had occasion to mention MODERNISM and REALISM and STRUCTURALISM in their lectures and with the same doubts I had. I had already written a book called *The Sun Rises in the Evening*, which deals with complementary opposites (monism and dualism) in an attempt to relate all humanistic culture; the time seemed right to look beyond literature, philosophy, and religion to other disciplines as well. So for six years, and while I tended to other projects, course work, and the exigencies of ordinary living, I read hundreds of books and articles, sent and received answers to numerous queries, and hopped from conference to conference in the United States, France, Germany, England, and Australia. As I went, I tried to restrict myself to key terms only (with as many others as are necessary to define the key terms) because I wanted to keep this book short enough to be read as any other book might. While it is intended primarily as a reference work, this glossary does argue a viewpoint, set out in the introduction, and I want the reader to be able to read it from cover to cover.

There are three principal parts to this glossary: a brief introductory essay suggesting links between the various disciplines; a glossary of hundreds of key terms from the various disciplines, from ABERRATION OF STARLIGHT to ZERO-SUM GAME; and a comprehensive guide to further study.

There are "dictionaries" similar to this glossary that nonetheless restrict themselves to modern developments only. There is no such restriction here; the present supplements the past as much as it invalidates it, and those who are familiar with Einstein and Sartre still refer to Aristotle and Kant. In the glossary I deal with both specific and general definitions (see CATEGORICAL IMPERATIVE or GRESHAM'S LAW, for example), multiple meanings of terms (DISPLACEMENT), and the application of terms in fields other than the field of origin (MÖBIUS STRIP). Where possible, I try to clear up misconceptions (as with FEEDBACK or SUBCONSCIOUS) and misapplications (MATERIALISM, NEGATIVE FEEDBACK). There is no strict scale to the individual entries; for example, there is more on SUPEREGO than on either EGO or ID simply because the former is a more resonant and provocative term. Within the entries, I have cited my authorities wherever necessary; some of the names refer to conversations or private correspondence, but for the most part, where I have written, for example, "as Lincoln Barnett says," the reader will be able to find in the Guide to Further Study a book or article that treats the term at greater length or possibly from a different angle.

Without too much exaggeration, it is fair to say that, above a certain level of mundane interaction, almost everyone I have encountered in the classroom or lecture hall over the past six years has helped me with this book. Among those who deserve special thanks are John Albright, Charles Anderson, William Bertrand, R. Bruce Bickley, Jr., David Bradley, Bonnie Braendlin, Douglas Fowler, Leon Golden, Hunt Hawkins, Kim Humiston, Susan Jeffords, David Jordan, Thomas A. Kirby, W. T. Lhamon, Jr., Edward Mendelson, Joe Nordgren, Greg Powell, Jerome Stern, Dennis Todd, and Dan White.

In addition to those who answered my questions and pointed me toward the right books and articles, three people deserve additional thanks for their involvement with the manuscript itself. The first is my wife, Barbara Hamby, a technical writer with a background in English and art history. The second is my colleague Hans Plendl, a nuclear physicist and leader of a popular graduate seminar in interdisciplinary studies at Florida State University. Like these two, my brother Albert Kirby, a physiologist and medical school professor, read drafts of the manuscript and showed me how it could be improved; it is to him that the book is dedicated.

# INTRODUCTION

At the extremes of our culture are two figures: the assassin talking himself into his act of violence, the devotee drowning himself in the vast sea of some cult. Between these two extremes the rest of us shift uneasily, wanting to be neither totally alone with ourselves nor totally lost in something outside. Consequently there is an unprecedented "hunger for wonders," as Theodore Roszak has called it in an essay entitled "In Search of the Miraculous"; wherever he goes, says Roszak, his audiences seem to ask if he has "a vision, an epiphany, an uncanny tale to relate? A moment of illumination or unearthly dread, a close encounter with arcane powers . . . ?"

One answer to this appetite for wonders is science fiction, with its emphasis on the future; another solution, and a more intellectually respectable one, is myth, which is rooted in the past. Thus biologist Paul Saltman writes, "We need a myth to live by, to bind us together in a civilization, to give us a morality, a set of values and concerns to share." This may be true, but it may not be possible. For one thing, myths relate supernatural events, and the supernatural will always have a tough time of it in a skeptical age. Since the Enlightenment, the drive has been toward analysis rather than synthesis, and analysis means the death of myth. Too, myths are anonymously authored; the deliberate creation of myth, then, is a contradiction in terms. Perhaps what is needed is not a myth but a metaphor, a very old metaphor, as it turns out, yet one that is given special meaning by our times.

When Sputnik I was launched on October 4, 1957, it changed the hearts and minds of a generation. Suddenly every schoolchild longed to be an astronaut. That meant more courses in physics and mathematics, fewer in chorus and home economics. In time, Sputnik's effects were mitigated. The hardening of the curriculum was reversed by the permissiveness of the late 1960s and early 70s (it made something of a comeback in the late 70s, though motivated this time by self-interest rather than fear of the Russians). Dreams of intergalactic space travel evaporated as the children who had those dreams grew into the realization that the technology necessary to carry them into the stellar depths was not going to develop as quickly as television and the movies promised and that, even if it did, they themselves were not ready for the thousand years' sleep that such voyages might entail. Members of the post-Sputnik generation went to graduate school, as planned, but settled into earthbound jobs.

Who are these children of space-age fantasy and mundane necessity? Imagine a youngish to middle-aged person of either sex, a resident of one of the industrialized nations, though not necessarily the one in which he or she was born, someone knowledgeable of the classics, schooled to some extent in science and mathematics (thanks to Sputnik), skilled above all in the use of words: possibly a writer of some kind, and certainly someone who reads, as Thomas Jefferson said of himself, "with a canine appetite." Skeptical of church and government, our representative person realizes that religion and politics express humankind's innate desire for the transcendent and that the rhetoric of each reveals a great deal about ordinary language and thus ordinary human needs and aspirations.

Members of the post-Sputnik generation are inclined to believe that literature represents the subtlest and most complex way to view reality, science the most precise. They recognize that they live in a plural world, a single entity viewed differently from the vantage points of myriad disciplines. Far from being disturbed by this proliferation and the attendant "danger" of overspecialization, they are refreshed by the variety of the plural world. Moreover, they know, if only at the intuitive level, that physicist and poet, chemist and craftsmen see the world in exactly the same way.

In the West, philosophy and science began in the sixth century B.C. with Thales, traditionally the first philosopher and scientist. One of the Seven Wise Men of Greece, Thales apparently wrote nothing but is credited with the utterance, "Everything is really water." This paradox expresses the ancient Greek notion that every object has at least some water in its composition, but since our five senses contradict that idea, clearly the statement means much more. Thales' statement says that there are really two worlds that are one and the same. First there is the apparent world, a world of great diversity that is perceived by our senses. But if everything in this world is really water, then in reality the world is a single entity and is not diverse at all. To put it another way, there is the apparent world perceived by our senses and the real world perceived through thought, both of which are one and the same. Why does not Thales say this? Because to explain away his own paradox would be to dilute its difficult yet undeniable implication: that the world is one and not-one simultaneously. (For a more thorough consideration of the Thalesian metaphor, see the first chapter of my book *The Sun Rises in the Evening: Monism and Quietism in Western Culture.*)

Notwithstanding the revolutions of Copernicus, Darwin, Freud, and Einstein, the Thalesian basis of science and philosophy—indeed, of all intellectual thought—is unchanged. The world is atomistic, it is holistic. It is atomistic in the sense that a cat and a bird are distinct, even opposed. But anyone who has seen a cat stalk a bird realizes that a whole cannot be explained solely in terms of the relation between its individual parts. If the cat were to approach the problem of catching the bird bit by bit, or atomistically, cats would have dropped out of the evolutionary chain long ago. Anyone who is familiar with poetry knows that one of its consistent functions from Homer forward is to create a bridge between our anxious perceptions of a broken world and our desires for one that is coherent and unified. In the modern world, Gestalt psychologists approach the individual functions of the human mind holistically, field physicists study bodies in terms of their gravitational and electromagnetic interactions with other bodies, visual artists work with discrete splashes and dabs of paint that form a harmonious whole. As various as these disciplines are, each is shaped by the understanding that this is a plural world, one and not-one at the same time.

We have seen others travel to the moon and back, but by now we know that, in cosmic terms, they have only been around the block. Our descendents may see space folk some day, but we won't, nor will our children, nor our children's children. Consequently, ethnocentrism has come back into fashion. There are more cultures in our crowded, tense world than the two described by C. P. Snow. There are dozens, hundreds. Each discipline is fractured into sub-disciplines, and each of these is walled off from the others by private languages and separate laws. In *Time of Need: Forms of Imagination in the Twentieth Century*, William Barrett says that

> a typical meeting of a university faculty today can sound like the clash of foreign tongues, each speaking from its own specialization with its particular assumptions, viewpoint, and very different body of information. Not only do scientists and humanists stand on different ground, but the scientists quarrel among themselves; sociologists may be at loggerheads with the economists, and psychologists with both; the schools of philosophers do not even condescend to try to understand each other; and even in mathematics, the universal language where unity of mind should be attained if anywhere, the quarrels among mathematicians provoked the great Poincaré to remark, *"Les hommes ne s'entendent pas parce qu'ils ne parlent pas la même langue."* ["Men do not agree because they do not speak the same language."] Our culture has brought down the tower of Babel from heaven to earth.

The more they understand of the different viewpoints, however, the more members of the post-Sputnik generation see that there are points of contact. There could be an underlying unity, they think, and thus a single earth-centered perspective from which all problems may be viewed. Perhaps Thales was right. Perhaps everything is really water.

But first we must agree. Poincaré's lament notwithstanding, it would be regrettable if we all spoke the same language. Cultural monolinguists will never know the "sweetness of miscellany" that novelist William Kennedy praises or the "thickness" that Jacques Barzun associates with William and Henry James, "the intense awareness of multiplicity—in nature, in persons, in art, religion, and social reality." The point is that we will never speak the same language, but with a little effort we can speak each other's languages; the following pages provide a start.

# DICTIONARY OF CONTEMPORARY THOUGHT

# A

***aberration of starlight***   An aberration is a straying from
the ideal (if the subject is morals) or the real (if it is optics). "Aberration of starlight" was discovered by eighteenth-
century English astronomer James Bradley and refers to the displacement of the path of light of a star. Everyone who has taken
eighth-grade science knows that shooting fish in a barrel is not as
easy as the adage suggests; the celebrated textbook illustration
shows that the actual fish is just below the image that the hunter
sees. The same is true with stars, though for a different reason.
The fish benefits from refraction: rays of light bend as they pass
from one medium to another because they change velocity, and
the eye is deceived. Starlight does not undergo the same
wrenching change in media, but it is seen at an angle because the
observer is rushing along the earth's orbit in a direction perpen-
dicular to the line of travel followed by the starlight. No telescope
is ever pointed toward the true position of a star, then. Only by
following a path that does not exist can the astronomer find what
he or she seeks.

   Gilbert Sorrentino's novel *Aberration of Starlight* presents a diverse group of corny, sexy, thoroughly mundane characters who
hop in and out of each other's lives in a New Jersey boardinghouse
during the Great Depression. The reader sees each one at different times and in different ways and is reminded that all fiction is
an angle into reality. Insofar as it is a description of what isn't
there, fiction is a lie that tells the truth. The master fabulist
Borges says that he is not a creator of fictions but an inventor of
facts.

**absolutism**   A total ironing out of the contraries, an annihilation of the uncertainties. Often absolutism necessitates a torpedo into one's past. When David Kepesh, the youthful protagonist of Philip Roth's *The Professor of Desire*, decides he would rather be a scholar than an actor, his drama-school friends mock him, but Kepesh says, "Well, I have my airs, and the power, apparently, to dramatize myself and my choices, but above all it is that I am an absolutist—a young absolutist—and know no way to shed a skin other than by inserting the scalpel and lacerating myself from end to end. I am one thing or I am the other."

**abstract expressionism**   First used in 1919 to describe the work of the Russian painter Kandinsky, the term reemerged in America after World War II. With its overriding emphasis on such purely "painterly" aspects as surface quality and brushstroke, abstract expressionism includes action painting as well as simple, reductive monoliths. Because of their notoriety, Jackson Pollock's enormous and violently spattered canvases have achieved near-cliché status as examples of abstract expressionism. But Mark Rothko's paintings, typically solid rectangles with subtle nuances of color that required months of preparation, belong to the same school. A student of Rothko named Ralph Pomeroy remarked once that the clean whites in some of Rothko's late work are "like silence. Like the intervals in Beethoven when there is no music."

Common to all abstract expressionism is the reminder that, as the Valéry poem says, God made the world from nothing, and from time to time the nothing shows through. Thus it may be that the ultimate motive of this school is suggested not so much by, say, a de Kooning drawing as by the specific de Kooning drawing that Robert Rauschenberg erased. Rauschenberg told Calvin Tomkins (in *Off the Wall*): "It was a drawing done partly with a hard line, and also with grease pencil, and ink, and heavy crayon. It took me a month, and about forty erasers, to do it."

**absurdity**   In the arts, a term describing the condition of the alienated individual in a meaningless world; often associated with

MODERNISM. In this sense the absurd came into being at the end of the nineteenth century. It was originally a comic mode and one with positive connotations, although it soon took on a grim cast. As Roger Shattuck notes, "Absence of any value becomes in itself a value. . . . Yet for all its philosophic implications, the absurd, during *la belle époque*, still provokes laughter, a quality it loses in the later skirmishes of, for instance, Kafka, André Breton, or Sartre."

One point about absurdity is that it is the norm in a godless world. In the nineteenth century, if someone were struck by lightning, the act would have been tragic, something called for in God's mysterious plan for us all. (See the general definition of TRAGEDY.) In current times, however, if humankind chooses to vaporize itself with nuclear warheads, the assumptions will be radically different. Instead of God blasting man in accordance with some long-term and ultimately beneficent scheme, man would be destroying himself to no end—an absurd action.

In drama, critic Martin Esslin has coined the phrase "theatre of the absurd." Samuel Beckett's *Waiting for Godot* (1955), a play in which two aged tramps wait for a Godlike figure who never comes, is the classic example.

**Acmeism** A movement in Russian poetry that began as a reaction against the mystical tendencies of SYMBOLISM. The Acmeists advocated, for example, the admiring of a rose for its beauty, not because it represented something; in this way Acmeism parallels IMAGISM. The movement included Anna Akmatova and Osip Mandelstam. It was suppressed along with other "decadent" movements in the arts in the 1920s.

**adaption-level principle** A psychological concept with roots in ancient philosophy, this principle argues the negative side of adaptability, since it says that we become tired of what we adapt to. The Stoics and Epicureans knew that self-perception and therefore happiness (and sorrow) are relative to our past experiences as well as our perception of the lot of others. If our present achievements fall below past ones or below the present achievements of others, we are disappointed, even if we only perceive this to be the case. Psychologists David Myers and Thomas Ludwig observe that a prosperous people may think of themselves as poor because their present prosperity is less than that of a previous decade; they have adapted to their times unhappily. The good becomes an evil or at least a boring neutrality. To take an example from another field, the color blue has a calming effect that has been established by laboratory experiments, but after a time a prisoner will adapt to the blue walls of a cell and become as restive as ever.

Compounding our tendency to adapt negatively is an innate feeling of superiority (again, established through experiments and surveys) that characterizes most people. This feeling gives rise to a sense that the ordinary compensation received by a member of any large group for his or her ordinary achievements is somehow less than it should be. In general, we receive what we deserve, although it does not seem that way. The fault is in the perception: as Myers and Ludwig point out, "The average person is *not* better than the average person."

**affective fallacy**   The mistake of judging something in terms of its results. W. K. Wimsatt Jr. and Monroe C. Beardsley define the affective fallacy as a confusion between what a poem is and what it does: "It begins by trying to derive the standard of criticism from the psychological effects of the poem and ends in impressionism and relativism." The audience becomes intoxicated on its feelings; the work disappears.

Wimsatt and Beardsley have taken some heat for their supposed unemotionalism. The epigraph to their essay is from an Eduard Hanslick essay on music; it says, "We might as well study the properties of wine by getting drunk," a caution that even the most ardent oenophile might spurn. But study, like the satisfaction of an appetite, has its place. Seeing precedes feeling. See INTENTIONAL FALLACY, NEW CRITICISM, and READER-RESPONSE CRITICISM.

**aleatory**   An adjective used in the arts to refer to compositional techniques that are at least partially dependent on chance or luck (in Latin *aleator* means "gambler"). The automatic drawing and writing of SURREALISM are aleatory, as is the action painting of Jackson Pollock (see ABSTRACT EXPRESSIONISM). In music, ATONALITY was unsystematic and therefore aleatory until Arnold Schönberg developed his theory of the twelve-tone row in the 1920s.

## Alexandrianism   See PRIMITIVISM.

## ambiguity   While "ambiguous" carries the pejorative meaning of "confused" or "muddled" in ordinary parlance, in the study of art and literature it can mean "susceptible to more than one interpretation," which is a plus. In *Seven Types of Ambiguity*, William Empson defines ambiguity as "any verbal nuance, however slight, which gives room for alternative reactions to the same piece of language." Useful to practitioners of the NEW CRITICISM and other close readers of poetry, ambiguity figures in other genres as well. For example, the novels of Henry James are often characterized as ambiguous because James frequently depicts characters who gain freedom (from a lover, say) at the expense of personal happiness. In such cases it is understandably difficult to speak of happy or unhappy endings.

## anoetic   A philosophical term referring to feelings that have not yet come to full cognition; opposed to NOETIC and similar in meaning to the psychological term PRECONSCIOUS.

## antimatter   In 1928 physicist P. A. M. Dirac predicted the existence of antimatter. In the words of Dirac's colleague Hans Plendl, "Since ordinary matter is made of positively charged protons and negatively charged electrons, why couldn't there also be matter that is made of *negatively* charged protons and *positively* charged electrons?" In 1932 the positron was discovered, the first known antiparticle; the antiproton was discovered in 1955 and the antineutron a year later. The existence of these antiparticles

made possible the creation of antimatter: whereas an atom consists of a nucleus composed of neutrons and protons with a net positive charge that is neutralized by the negatively charged electrons that orbit it, an atom of antimatter consists of a nucleus composed of antineutrons and antiprotons with a net negative charge that is neutralized by orbiting positrons. Such "antiatoms" would be necessarily shortlived in our world because they would be quickly annihilated by conventional matter, but in theory there is no reason to doubt the possibility of entire worlds of antimatter far from our own. Since the basic physical unit is known to exist, however tenuously, then so does the potential for larger forms.

**antimodernism**   In the arts, a return to traditional themes and forms; a reaction to MODERNISM. Graham Hough notes that in modern times revolutions succeed all too rapidly. "Modernist techniques soon become familiar, become boring," says Hough. "So they produce a reaction. Hence the rise of a fairly conscious anti-modernism of the next generation [i.e., the generation after Eliot and Joyce]; Graham Greene, Waugh, Auden and his followers, the enhanced reputations of Robert Graves and Hardy, in the doldrums after the modernist triumph. This in its turn wears out and a new modernism comes back."

**antinomianism**   Touched by grace, an antinomian does not have to answer to the prevailing authorities (in Greek *nomos* means "law"). Antinomianism is a tenet of GNOSTICISM, and in the decades following Christ's death the gnostics were a thorn in the side of the Church fathers. But by the Middle Ages, what had been a form of dissent became, at least on the part of some gnostic groups, an open door to sexual license and other behavior that was socially as well as morally objectionable. Hence one difficulty with antinomianism: once outside the confines of moral law, it is easy for the permissible to become the permissive, the self-indulgent, even the self-destructive. The other difficulty is that antinomian behavior may be wrongly perceived by the orthodox as not merely different but actually threatening. When mainstream Christianity allied itself with the military establishment, sometime after

Constantine converted to Christianity in the fourth century, heresy became not only an inadvisable but often a fatal enterprise.

Today antinomianism has a strong secular definition. For example, someone who considers himself too spiritual to work for a living is an antinomian.

**antinovel**   Any novel written in protest against the dominant novel form of its day; of necessity an experimental or avant-garde novel. Thus Cervantes's *Don Quixote* (1605) and Sterne's *Tristram Shandy* (1759) are antinovels, as is the NOUVEAU ROMAN of this century.

**apriorism**   *A priori* knowledge is not derived from experience and is therefore certain; two and two always make four. *A posteriori*, or empirical, knowledge is derived from experience and involves probability rather than certainty; most squirrels are gray, though some are albino. On a higher level, apriorism admits metaphysical and moral principles as well. For example, we do not need to be told that it is wrong to commit suicide because that knowledge is innate within us. In the broadest sense, an apriorist is one who believes that much can be learned from pure thought with no recourse to experience.

**archetype**   According to Jung, the collective unconscious, the racial memory, is populated with "primordial images" or archetypes. Quoting Jung and then elaborating, Maud Bodkin notes that these archetypes are " 'psychic residua of numberless experiences of the same type,' experiences which have happened not to the individual but to his ancestors, and of which the results are inherited in the structure of the brain, *a priori* determinants of individual experience." These archetypes inform our myths, religions, folklore, dreams, fantasies, and literature; an example is the sphinxlike creature that drags itself through the desert in Yeats's "The Second Coming."

Somewhat self-protectively, T.S. Eliot remarked that "the prelogical mentality persists in civilized man, but becomes available only to or through the poet." Gilbert Murray (also quoted by Bodkin) addressed the matter more democratically and with a greater sense of the magic of archetypes when he wrote, "In plays like *Hamlet* or the *Agamemnon* or the *Electra* we have certainly fine and flexible character study, a varied and well-wrought story, a full command of the technical instruments of the poet and the dramatist; but we have also, I suspect, a strange, unanalysed vibration below the surface, an undercurrent of desires and fears and passions, long slumbering yet eternally familiar, which have for thousands of years lain near the root of our most intimate emotions and been wrought into the fabric of our most magical dreams. How far into past ages this stream may reach back, I dare not even surmise; but it seems as if the power of stirring it or moving with it were one of the last secrets of genius." See APRIORISM and COLLECTIVE UNCONSCIOUS.

**art brut**    French "raw art"; the spontaneous and crude art of such nonprofessionals as children, vandals, and the mentally disturbed. The phrase was coined by the French painter and sculptor Jean Dubuffet and is extended to cover professional artwork that is deliberately childlike and primitive, like Dubuffet's own.

**art deco**    A decorative style with links to FUTURISM, art deco emulates modern industrial design in its use of long, thin forms and straight lines. It was popular in the 1920s and 30s and again in the 1970s. Such "stepped-back" skyscrapers as the Chrysler Building offer architectural examples of art deco.

**artificial intelligence**    Also machine intelligence, or simply AI. Christopher Evans traces the beginning of the need for AI to the 1880 U.S. census. Never an easy task, census taking had become a near-impossibility following the great waves of immigration to this country in the last half of the nineteenth century. When the Census Bureau realized in 1887 that the 1880 figures were still uncounted, three conclusions were reached. One, the results, when derived, would be hopelessly out of date; two, the next census, which would have to deal with even more people, would pose even greater problems; and three, there had to be a better way of dealing with the raw figures already gathered. So a competition was held. Loony suggestions abounded, but in the end three finalists were put to a practical test of data processing. One William C. Hunt (who used colored cards) finished the exercise in 55 hours, and a certain Charles F. Pidgin (who used colored tokens) took 44 hours. The third competitor and the one least favored by the oddsmakers was Herman Hollerith, inventor of a machine that scanned punched cards. Hollerith's machine finished the problem in 5½ hours and was selected for the 1890 census. The data from that census were tabulated in a record six weeks (the population then was 62,622,250), and Hollerith said with pride and accuracy, "I am the first statistical engineer." He founded the Tabulating Machine Company, now I.B.M.

In World War II, British intelligence gave AI a push forward out of necessity. The hopeless underdog in military terms, Britain got by with her wits—and her computers, which served many uses but were crucial to the code-cracking that provided the Allies with the foreknowledge of so many German operations. In the Cold War period, computers were used on a broader scale, for instance, to map defense strategies and in the space race. Finally, as computer techniques were applied to business problems, sheer commercialism turned the computer industry into what it is today. And what it is will determine what we are, says Evans, who goes so far as to predict that the computer will be responsible for the decline and fall of communism. The computer revolution, as Evans calls it, will lead to unprecedented affluence in capitalist countries, the only ones that provide the incentive for breakneck technological advance. The communist countries, already a decade or more behind in computer technology, will witness ruefully the restructuring of society. It will be a peaceful and rapid restructuring, bloodless, and founded on cheap, universally available computer power.

For the moment, computers exist that can beat all but a handful of the world's best chess players. "And if this does not make you feel the computer's hot breath on your neck," says Evans, "then nothing will." It will not be long before the computer represents more than a superior chess partner, and, surprisingly, those jobs thought least susceptible to automated replacement may be the first to go, and vice versa. It is the unskilled who are safe; people will still be needed to deliver a package or pack an instrument for shipping. But advancements in AI will mean that much more teaching will be done by computers in the future as well as various kinds of screening and interviewing previously done by professionals; it has already been determined that people are franker when confiding physical or emotional problems to a neutral computer keyboard than they would be if they had to face a possibly disapproving doctor or psychologist. And before the reader objects to such "dehumanized" developments, Evans asks if there is anyone who insists that paralytics would be better off if they had to depend on the muscular effort of round-the-clock crews rather than on the iron lungs that keep them breathing efficiently and cheaply.

As AI affects us increasingly, will we fall in love with the computers that make our lives more and more pleasant? Unfortunately, some of us already have; university physicians are reporting that certain students have better relationships with their computers than with their more fallible peers. (Steven Levy says the student fanatic "gets itchy, gets tired of the illogical bumps and tangents of human conversation. There's almost a physical yearning for the machine." And he quotes the director of a computer facility at Stanford as saying, " 'Who else do you know who will do whatever you tell it to do?' ") We may pity these students now, but it may be that computers will become more truly lovable as time goes by. Douglas R. Hofstadter says that emotions cannot be directly programmed into a machine but that as AI develops they will occur naturally, like human emotions, "which arise indirectly from the organization of our minds. Programs or machines will acquire emotions in the same way: as by-products of their structure, of the way in which they are organized—not by direct programming."

Neither Evans nor Hofstadter broaches the mind-arresting possibility of sex between humans and computers, but chances are that the machines will want us to keep that sort of thing to ourselves. Evans expresses his view of the future by summarizing a story by A. E. Van Vogt called *The Human Operators*. The *dramatis personae* of this tale are spaceships that have been given a high degree of AI in order to carry out a routine exploration of the solar system. But human error has made the ships a little too smart, and they decide to become independent. They scatter to the far corners of the universe, rendezvousing every two or three decades in order to mate their crews. These "human operators" soon forget their origins and go about those necessary, irreplaceable maintenance tasks mentioned earlier while the ships do whatever it is that they do, whatever they want.

John R. Searle sees stories like these as part of a prevailing and temporary mythology about computers. A computer can be programmed to print out the request "Please give me a drink," but who would take that to mean that a machine can be literally thirsty? Similarly, a computer might be able to manipulate foreign words and phrases well enough to fool a native, but that does not mean it would attribute meaning or content to the terms any more than a pocket calculator understands what it is doing when it adds two and two. Searle explains the mindlessness of computers by asking the reader to imagine a person who doesn't understand Chinese in a room with a rule book and a box of ideograms that he passes back and forth to people outside the room so expertly that the outsiders think the human "computer" is fluent in Chinese, a language of which he understands nothing but is only manipulating according to his rule book or "program."

We tend to romanticize the unfamiliar, Searle suggests, and "until computers and robots become as common as cars and until people are able to program and use them as easily as they now drive cars we are likely to continue to suffer from a certain mythological conception of the computer." See BINARY SYSTEM.

**art nouveau**   A sensuous and richly ornamental style that emerged in Europe in the 1880s. Art nouveau is seen in the erotic drawings of Aubrey Beardsley, in the ornate wrought-iron entrances of some Paris *métro* stations, and in the psychedelic posters of the 1960s.

**assemblage**   See COLLAGE.

**atonality**   The avoidance of key in music and therefore the avoidance of music's natural tendency toward consonance; deliberately dissonant music. It is sometimes said that an audience knows when a tonal work is over because the music returns to the point where it began, hovers harmonically for a few moments, and ends on a tonic chord, whereas the audience knows for certain that an atonal work is over only when the conductor puts down the baton, turns, and bows.

The progress of Western music from tonality to the atonal works of composers like Arnold Schönberg and Charles Ives has prompted William Barrett to ponder in *Time of Need* the transition from "the gracious concords of polyphony" to "the intricate harmonies of diatonic music" to "cacaphonous polytonality" to, finally, "the homeless voice of atonality." It is "a rather startling sequence," writes Barrett, "as if Mozart were to break down and stammer in the incoherent fragments of Samuel Beckett's Lucky and then at last become silent." Yet who would have arrested this process, and at what point? To do so would see the music that dominated at the point of arrest kill itself off through sheer repetition. Barrett is saying that the lot of the serious avant-garde artist is always a difficult one, caught "between the Scylla of aesthetic stagnation and the Charybdis of empty experimentation." See ALEATORY.

# B

**baroque**   An artistic style that flourished mainly in the seventeenth century and that was marked by the extravagant, the elaborate, sometimes even the grotesque. At its height, the baroque style is exemplified by Bernini's sculpture of the ecstasy of St. Teresa. See ROCOCO.

**Bauhaus**   See CONSTRUCTIVISM.

**Bayes's theorem**   Your team is bigger, faster, and healthier; their team is smaller, slower, and injury-ridden. It stands to reason, then, that you should take a second mortgage on the house and bet on your own players, especially since they have the advantage of playing on the home field. When the halftime score is 62-0 in the other team's favor, however, and you are frantically trying to arrange a third mortgage in order to bet against yourself, you are only invoking Bayes's theorem (or Bayes's rule, after eighteenth-century English clergyman and mathematician Thomas Bayes), which says that hypotheses held before an experiment should be modified in light of the results. The limitation of Bayes's theorem is that it applies only to situations where some *a priori* knowledge is available (if you know nothing about the other team, no hypothesis, even an incorrect one, is possible). An example of the application of Bayes's theorem in medical science involves exercise testing to diagnose heart disease. The doctor typically finds certain changes in the electrocardiogram as the subject runs on a

treadmill. In a younger person these changes are of no significance, whereas in an older subject the changes are indicative of
coronary artery disease; therefore the observations must be fac-
tored to account for the age of the subject. See INDUCTION and
SINGULARITY.


**behaviorism**    In its purest form, behaviorism rejects any
concern with the invisible aspects of mind and deals only with observable response to stimuli, to reward and punishment. Gordon
Rattray Taylor says that when J.B. Watson introduced behaviorism in 1913 he insisted that the word "consciousness" be dropped
from the vocabulary. The mind is a black box: stimuli go in, behavior comes out, and what goes on in the box is of no importance. The
Russian Pavlov was even more fanatical, says Taylor, and would
fine his students if they used the words "mind" or "mental." A
striking area of interest in this regard is language development.
Behaviorists believe that language develops as the spontaneous
babblings of the infant are rewarded appropriately (or not) by the
parent; this hypothesis is disputed by Noam Chomsky and others,
who postulate an inherent neurological awareness of the basic elements of language structure.

Some opponents of behaviorism are fond of emphasizing its potential use by totalitarian regimes, pointing out that Pavlov
reached such favor with the Soviets that they built a laboratory
for him in 1935. More to the point, the antibehaviorists betray an
insatiable curiosity to know just what is going on in that black box
of the mind. According to William Barrett (in *The Illusion of
Technique*), behaviorists would say that the telescope was invented because Galileo received a stimulus (he heard that a
Dutchman had made an enlarging glass) that elicted a response
(he invented the telescope). What this formula overlooks is
Galileo's celebrated "night of prolonged meditation," which
occurred after he heard the news from the Netherlands but before
he had come up with his own invention. The more we know about
what happened during the long hours of that night, says Barrett,
the more we know, period. He quotes novelist Iris Murdoch's con-
demnation of the narrowness of the behaviorist view, which describes only the world "in which people play cricket, cook cakes,

make simple decisions, remember their childhood, and go to the circus; not the world in which they commit sins, fall in love, say prayers, or join the Communist party." And Taylor cites a social psychologist who laments: "I am sadly aware of my own inability to capture even remotely the wonder that mind is, especially when I think of such products of mind as the Fifth Symphony, the Sermon on the Mount, *The Brothers Karamazov*, or the calculus. Whatever it is that enables mind to create and to appreciate such marvels seems to elude almost completely the crude nets of any psychological jargon." No doubt the behaviorists would offer their methods as a counter to such jargon, and certainly behaviorism is praiseworthy insofar as it is an antidote to useless speculation. Too, behavioral techniques are highly effective in the treatment of common anxieties whose origins are complex yet whose manifestations are simple and easily checked; an example is the use of relaxation techniques to control anger. See HUMANISTIC PSYCHOLOGY.

**Bell's theorem**   In a paper entitled "Bell's Theorem and World Process," Berkeley physicist H. P. Stapp says, "Bell's theorem is the most profound discovery of science"; three pages later, Stapp says that the theorem is "incomprehensible in the framework of ordinary ideas." Perhaps the easiest way to describe Bell's theorem (published by physicist J. S. Bell in 1964) is to say that it contradicts the PRINCIPLE OF LOCAL CAUSES and suggests instead a "quantum interconnectedness," in which particles that were once in contact continue to influence each other, no matter how far apart—in Amaury de Riencourt's words, "Distant entities in the universe can apparently act as parts of a greater whole." If this is so, then, as Stapp says in "S-Matrix Interpretation of Quantum Theory," Bell's theorem shows that "our most ordinary ideas about the world are somehow profoundly deficient even on the macroscopic level."

**big-bang theory**   Once on an equal footing with the steady-state theory, the big-bang theory is now accepted by most scientists. The big-bangers maintain that all matter and energy existed once in a form that was concentrated and, to put it mildly, extremely hot—trillions of degrees, according to Robert Jastrow. Then came an explosion, about 20 billion years ago, which dispersed this matter and energy throughout the universe. This model is disputed by the steady-staters, who argue that new material is constantly being created. Such an assertion defies the law of conservation of energy (see CONSERVATION LAWS), but the steady-staters say that laws formulated in laboratories may not apply in the dark reaches of the universe. Recent work with radio telescopes has given the nod to the big-bang theory, however. For example, it has been proven that galaxies and quasars (quasistellar objects) are less numerous and less intense than they were in the past, suggesting that the basic components of the universe are both finite and diminishing, as the big-bang theory suggests. (As with so many other concepts, it would be more accurate to speak of the big-bang theories, since there are variations on the basic model described here.)

If this is how the universe began, then how will it end, and how does speculation about the end help us refine our knowledge about the beginning? At least three basic scenarios suggest themselves. First, the universe could simply continue to expand, grow emptier, darker, and cooler, then cease to exist altogether. Second, it could stop expanding and start contracting because of gravitational pull. Third, some combination of the first two scenarios is possible, though with consequences that are difficult to foresee, in which parts of the universe continue to expand while others contract. Recent measurements tentatively favor the first and third scenarios; apparently there is not enough matter in the universe to exert a gravitational attraction strong enough to reverse the expansion of its parts. It will be difficult for scientists of a religious, philosophical, or poetic bent to let go of the second scenario, however. As Robert Jastrow points out, this model combines the ideas of the finite creation (the initial fiery explosion lasted only a few hours) and the infinite universe, because the universe would be compacted and remade out of its present components (though so utterly changed that no trace of the universe we know now will exist). There will be a second creation, a third, and so on.

To understand the skepticism of most contemporary scientists toward this attractive yet unlikely scenario is to understand as well their earlier skepticism toward any sort of big-bang theory. Einstein himself preferred the steady-state concept for many years, sharing with his colleagues the desire for an ageless, unchanging universe. Many scientists are unhappy with the idea of a finite beginning since it forces them to ponder what existed before the known universe did. That question has disturbing theological implications, especially since it cannot be answered. Jastrow notes that we can see back 15 billion years or so, since quasars have been photographed at distances of 15 billion years—but no farther, because of an obscuring fog of radiation that was generated by the original explosion and dispersed only after several billion years. Thus "science will never be able to raise the curtain on the mystery of creation. For the scientist who has lived by his faith in the power of reason, the story ends like a bad dream. He has scaled the mountains of ignorance; he is about to conquer the highest peak; as he pulls himself over the final rock, he is greeted by a band of theologians who have been sitting there for centuries." See HUBBLE'S LAW, INFLATIONARY UNIVERSE, and RED SHIFT.

**binary system** Mathematical system based on only two digits, 0 and 1, in contrast to the more familiar decimal system. The first ten numbers in binary notation are 0 (0), 1 (1), 10 (2), 11 (3), 100 (4), 101 (5), 110 (6), 111 (7), 1000 (8), and 1001 (9). The binary system complicates ordinary computation, since the binary equivalent of the number 17, expressed with two digits, is the five-digit 10001. (Binary numbers are sometimes written with a subscript $_b$ to distinguish them from decimal numbers in order that, to use the example just given, $10001_b$ not be mistaken for a much higher 10001.) But the simplicity of the system makes it crucial to computer operation, since a binary digit can be signaled by the mere presence or absence of an electrical charge.

It is interesting to note that Leibniz, who developed an early calculating machine of sorts, was for a time fascinated with the binary system. What would have happened, asks Christopher Evans, if Leibniz had combined these two interests—"giant steam-driven computers in the nineteenth century," say, and "the beginning of the Industrial Revolution fifty years ahead of its time and in Germany instead of Britain?" One may speculate endlessly but futilely, for Leibniz never put two and two, or $10_b$ and $10_b$, together.


**black-body radiation**   A black object neither reflects nor emits light unless heated. Thus black-body radiation is a pure form of radiation, ideal for laboratory study. In the course of his research into the nature of black-body radiation, Max Planck made the discovery that light is emitted and absorbed not continuously, but in small packets. This discovery was the first step in the development of QUANTUM MECHANICS.


**black box**   An engineering term referring to any sealed device whose internal workings are inaccessible, "black box" is also used by philosophers and psychologists of certain schools (e.g., BEHAVIORISM) to describe the human brain.


**black hole**   The last possible stage in the life of a star. When a star can no longer exert sufficient expansive force and begins to succumb to the compressive force of its own gravitation, it starts to shrink in size and increase in density. Along the way, the shrinking star may assume a stable configuration and become a white dwarf. But if it continues to compress, the star will become a black hole, a region in which gravitational pull is so strong that no light can escape. This means that a black hole cannot be observed directly; its existence can only be predicated on its effect on nearby bodies. See EVENT HORIZON and STELLAR EVOLUTION.


**Boolean algebra**   See SYMBOLIC LOGIC.


**Brownian movement**   The incessant, irregular motion of tiny particles suspended in a liquid; named for eighteenth-century botanist Robert Brown, who observed the motion of spores in water. The spores moved because of the buffeting they took from the molecules of the water.

The importance of Brown's discovery is that it substantiates the molecular nature of all matter, which is composed of particles (molecules) that are in constant motion.


**bruitisme** See FUTURISM.

# C

**catastrophe theory**   Catastrophe theory is concerned with events that occur abruptly, from an earthquake to a nervous breakdown. In their study of dynamic systems that pass through points of instability, catastrophe theorists point out that everything in nature has a breaking point that can be reached simply by bringing to bear a mathematically determinable amount of force, causing the catastrophe.

**catastrophism**   The theory that natural catastrophes have caused massive extinctions of plant and animal life. An examination of the fossil record suggests at least six such catastrophes, including one 65 million years ago that destroyed 75 percent of existing plant and animal species, including dinosaurs, leaving no land animal weighing more than 55 pounds. Geologist Walter Alvarez, discovering 30 times the normal concentration of the element iridium in a layer of Italian limestone that would have been laid down at about the time the dinosaurs died out, concluded that an asteroid 10 kilometers in diameter had struck the earth. Since iridium is rare in earth rocks but is 1,000 times more prevalent in asteroids, Alvarez hypothesizes that the asteroid may have thrown up enough iridium-rich rock and dust to cut off sunlight for a period of several months, during which the plants on which the dinosaurs and other animals fed were destroyed. This catastrophe, as well as others that have been suggested (such as a massive volcanic eruption), could also have created a greenhouse effect by generating enough water vapor to warm the earth and make it impossible for the various species to reproduce.

While the fossil record shows that the last catastrophe occurred 6–10,000 years ago (when most giant mammals were eliminated, including mastodons, mammoths, and ground sloths), presumably what has happened may happen again.

**categorical imperative**   The categorical imperative, or absolute (as opposed to conditional) moral law, is sometimes described as a sophisticated version of the Golden Rule, and not without justification. Kant formulated the categorical imperative in his *Critique of Pure Reason*, in which he urges the reader to act as though the principle underlying his action were to become a universal law.

**catharsis**   From the Greek "cleansing." Freud urged the cathartic method early in the belief that if he urged a patient enough the patient would articulate a specific trauma that lay behind the disturbance. As he became more skilled in analysis, however, Freud realized that neurotic states often originated in conflict rather than in trauma and that he could obtain better results by allowing his patient to engage in free association, saying whatever came to mind with no direction from the analyst, wandering finally into the unconscious mind and discovering there the anxiety-producing conflict. Ernest Jones, Freud's biographer, locates the true beginning of psychoanalysis in Freud's transition from the cathartic to the free-association method.

**cathexis**   In psychoanalysis, the investment of psychic energy in someone or something to the point of fixation. In "Reflections: Freud and the Soul," Bruno Bettelheim complains that this is one of the many Freudian terms that have a simple German equivalent (in this case, *Besetzung* or "occupation") but that are given annoying and incomprehensible equivalents in English. The German *Besetzung* suggests correctly a military-style occupation, a forceful commitment of energies that hampers or halts normal functions. Since psychoanalysis seeks to make known the unknown, Freud was reportedly unhappy with this and similar errors of judgment on the part of his English translators.

**causality**   The relation of a cause to its specific effect. In general, it is accepted that a given stimulus will produce identical results if administered under controlled conditions. However, acceptance of the various implications of the principle of causality is not automatic among scientists. David Hume argued that there was no internal bond between any two phenomena; if fire exists, so does heat, but one does not necessarily bring the other into existence. In *The Illusion of Technique,* William Barrett says that "the notion of cause or force as an occult power or inner bond between phenomena was to be banished from the physical sciences. Science states only the co-presence and co-variation of facts within the world." Hence the reluctance of some scientists to argue cause and effect, even with respect to matters as seemingly obvious as the toxicity of cigarette smoke: rather than say smoking causes cancer, one might argue that cancer-prone people tend to smoke. For a discussion of acausality in modern physics, see HIDDEN-VARIABLE THEORY and QUANTUM MECHANICS.

**classicism**   In its ideal form, a reflection of the great traditions of the Greeks and Romans with their characteristic emphasis on order, clarity, simplicity, moderation, systematic thinking; in its degenerate form, intellectual sterility and narrowness of outlook—Brahminism, in a word. Classical attitudes enjoyed splendid resurgences during the Renaissance and in the eighteenth century, sometimes referred to as the neoclassical period.

**cognitive consonance**   Consistency in a cognitive system; its opposite is cognitive dissonance. An example of the former would be a moderation of one's drinking habits following the issuance of a government report linking alcohol consumption and disease. But cognitive dissonance would characterize the behavior of someone who continued to drink heavily and blamed the government report on hostility toward the alcohol industry. Cognitive dissonance can be applied positively, of course, as in the case of someone who concludes that he has developed certain strengths of character from being born with a handicap. (In this example, cognitive consonance might result in feelings of despair and self-pity.)

**cognitive dissonance** See COGNITIVE CONSONANCE.

**collage** The artistic technique of gluing flat objects to a surface; from the French "pasting." ("Assemblage" refers to a similar use of three-dimensional objects.) Paintings with glued-on objects appear in every phase of history, but it was not until the twentieth century that collage became a major art form, affecting the development of CUBISM and other movements.

**collective unconscious** In addition to our individual UNCONSCIOUS, Jung posits a collective unconscious that is the same from person to person. "Although we human beings have our own personal life," he writes, "we are yet in large measure the representatives, the victims and promoters of a collective spirit whose years are counted in centuries." We may think that "we are following our own noses," according to Jung, "and may never discover that we are, for the most part, supernumeraries on the stage of the world theater. There are factors which, although we do not know them, nevertheless influence our lives, the more so if they are unconscious."

With respect to our being victims of the collective unconscious, John Maynard Keynes said the "practical men who believe themselves to be quite exempt from any intellectual influences are usually the slaves of some defunct economist." This is a handy, all-purpose dictum, since one can substitute "astronomer" or "football coach" or any other title for "economist" and apply it to any endeavor whatsoever.

Student poets sometimes resist the study of their tradition, saying that a conscious knowledge of past poetry can only confine their own original expression. What is odd is that so many of these novices are writing precisely the same poem, totally independent of each other. The poem is usually in quatrains, is end-rhymed in an AABB pattern, is in iambic tetrameter or some slight variation thereon, and has a first-person speaker: "I think that I shall never see / A poem as lovely as a tree," and so on. See APRIORISM and ARCHETYPE.

**commutative mathematics**   In a commutative operation, the combination of two elements does not depend on the order in which the elements are combined. E.g., in simple multiplication, $2 \times 4 = 8$, and so does $4 \times 2$.

In noncommutative mathematics, the order of the elements affects the results. Thus the multiplication of matrices (rectangular arrangements of numbers) and vectors (quantities having both magnitude and direction) are noncommutative.

**complementarity**   Given the fact that light has wave characteristics at certain times and particle characteristics at others, Niels Bohr argued in 1927 that light is of a complementary nature. Light cannot be both wavelike and particlelike simultaneously, yet one must understand the behavior of both waves and particles if one is to understand the behavior of light rays. Bohr extends this idea to cover duality in any phenomenon, saying that an experiment that successfully studies a single aspect of a system will obscure that aspect's complement. A second physicist, Wolfgang Pauli, makes a similar kind of statement: "I can choose to observe one experimental set-up, A, and ruin B, or chose to observe B and ruin A. I cannot choose not to ruin one of them." As with GÖDEL'S THEOREM and the UNCERTAINTY PRINCIPLE, the complementarity principle sets a limit to what humankind can know and control.

**complex**   A term originated by C.G. Jung to indicate a nexus of repressed ideas that underly some specific neurotic disorder; see REPRESSION.

**conceptualism**  As with MINIMALISM, conceptualism moves away from skill and dexterity in the arts and toward an intellectual rather than a sensual appeal. But whereas minimalism may still deal with objects, conceptualism dispenses with them altogether and offers slogans, handwritten notes, and other verbal or iconographic signs as a substitute for the representational.

For a definition of philosophic conceptualism, see NOMINALISM.

**conscious**  The state of awareness; the mental state characterized primarily by the functioning of the EGO. For one provocative account of the origin of consciousness, see SPLIT-BRAIN ANALYSIS. See also UNCONSCIOUS.

**conservation laws**  Principles that state that in any closed system the total amount of any quantity (e.g., mass or energy) remains constant, even though it may assume different forms. See BIG-BANG THEORY.

**constancy principle**  The tendency toward stability, according to Freud's biographer Ernest Jones. Freud himself wrote in *Beyond the Pleasure Principle* that "if the work of the mental apparatus is directed towards keeping the quantity of excitation low, then anything that is calculated to increase that quantity is bound to be felt as adverse to the functioning of the apparatus, that is, unpleasurable." Thus the PLEASURE PRINCIPLE derives from the constancy principle (occasionally referred to by Jones as the "constancy-nirvana principle").

**constructivism**  Art movement in Russia that flourished in the 1920s. Derived from the principles of CUBISM and FUTURISM, constructivism developed along the lines of social utilitarianism and came to international importance mainly through its influence on the German Bauhaus school of art and architecture with its severely functional designs. At its peak, constructivism was officially discouraged along with other modern art movements in

Russia, just as the Bauhaus school was banned in Germany in the 1930s. See also CUBO-FUTURISM.

### convergent infinite series   See INFINITE SERIES.

### correlation   A statistical method involving variables that are related but not dependent (compare with REGRESSION). For example, there is a correlation between stature in siblings; if your sister is tall, you are likely to be tall, but if she has an accident and loses her legs, you are not likely to undergo an equivalent reduction in height.

Correlation is important to social and political surveys. An example of multiple correlation would be an analysis of opinions on some controversial issue (such as abortion rights or handgun control) as correlated with age, sex, income, and so on; presumably one of these correlates would be stronger than the others, allowing activists to identify and concentrate on one highly susceptible group and not waste their resources on groups likely to be recalcitrant or indifferent.

### countertransference   See TRANSFERENCE.

### critical mass   The minimum quantity of nuclear fuel needed for a chain reaction to start.

### cubism   An arts movement concerned with highly stylized and often geometric forms; its leaders were Pablo Picasso and Georges Braque. As with IMPRESSIONISM, cubism takes its name from a hostile critic, in this case one who jeered at the "little cubes" of which these painters seemed so fond. Roger Shattuck makes an important distinction between artistic theory and practice, noting that cubism was not a "rigid doctrine" and instead had about it always a "probationary nature. . . . The high spirits that produced cubism acted as a safeguard in a manner lost sight of to-

day because of the unrelieved seriousness with which cubism is treated. The enjoyment of a good hoax—insofar as it was a hoax—prevented most painters from capitulating totally to the theoretical side of the school." See CUBO-FUTURISM.


**cubo-futurism**   Russian arts movement of the 1910s. Derived from CUBISM and FUTURISM, it eventually turned into CONSTRUCTIVISM.


**cybernetics**   Mathematician Norbert Wiener founded this interdisciplinary science of control systems, according to which constant FEEDBACK causes constant changes in the function of systems as disparate as a cooling system (which responds to the urgings of a thermostat) and a car-and-driver (which responds somewhat more complexly to unforeseen road conditions, the driver's routine patterns as altered by occasional whim, and so on).

This second example illustrates the effect that cybernetics has had on the classical perception of the dichotomy between organic and inorganic systems. With its widespread applicability to economics, ecology, engineering, and so on, cybernetics is, according to the *Harper Dictionary of Modern Thought*, best thought of as "the science of effective organization." See INFORMATION THEORY and SYSTEM.

# D

**Dada**  A movement in the arts that has its roots in NIHILISM and that ultimately became the basis for SURREALISM; its founder was the poet Tristan Tzara. Originating in Zurich in 1916, Dada reflected disillusionment and tried deliberately to offend with its incoherent forms, its repetition of nonsense syllables ("dada" itself is a nonsense word), and its pretense that manufactured objects were art, as with the urinal entitled *Fountain* by Marcel Duchamp and exhibited as a work of sculpture. "The original Dadas were primarily *against* things," writes Calvin Tomkins in *Off the Wall*, "against politics, against European culture, against art both past and present." See READY-MADE.

**dandyism**  See DECADENCE.

**death instinct**  See REPETITION-COMPULSION.

**decadence**  In art, a period of diminishing standards, often one in which content becomes less important than form and technique is refined at the expense of subject matter. A frequent complaint about decadent periods is that they are self-reflexive, resulting in poems about poems, films about films, and so on.

This emphasis on art for art's sake characterizes a late nineteenth-century group called the Decadents, represented by writers like Oscar Wilde and artists like Aubrey Beardsley and memorialized in such novels as Wilde's *The Picture of Dorian Gray* (1891) and J. K. Huysmans's *A Rebours* (1884). In this century the influence of the Decadents is seen in the aggressive dandyism described in Evelyn Waugh's *Brideshead Revisited* (1945).

**Decadents, the**   See DECADENCE.

**decline effect**   A diminution in performance from the beginning to the end of an experiment. Arthur Koestler cites the decline effect in extrasensory-perception experiments. Since the LAW OF GREAT NUMBERS requires a large number of instances in ESP experiments, subjects find themselves making thousands of guesses over periods of months or weeks. Toward the end of these monotonous sessions, subjects tend to become less and less accurate, and after long periods of time most of them lose their special powers entirely.

**deduction**   Reasoning from the general to the particular; the use of a law or rule to predict the outcome of a given case. Dropped objects fall; thus if I release this pencil, it will end up on the floor. Deductive reasoning is definitive and absolute, says Warren Weaver, and for it we have the Greeks to thank, "who first saw clearly . . . the great power of announcing general axioms or assumptions and deducing from these a useful array of implied propositions." In a secondary and less formal sense, deduction means arriving at a conclusion that follows necessarily from stated premises; thus Sherlock Holmes knows that a badly scratched watch case was owned by a drunk who marred its surface in his inebriated attempts to insert the winding key. See INDUCTION and SYLLOGISM.

**deconstruction**   Whether this form of literary criticism is, to borrow Vincent B. Leitch's words, "a nihilistic ungraspable threat" or "an outright enlivening challenge" is debatable. What is certain is the uneasy feeling that creeps over one who must describe coherently a technique of deliberate incoherence. According to Kenneth L. Woodward and others, deconstruction begins by denying plot, theme, subject. Thus *Hamlet* is neither mystery nor tragedy nor character study. Instead it is an "impersonal skein" of arbitrary linguistic codes and conventions that anyone can read in any way. Jacques Derrida, the high priest of deconstruction, distinguishes between conversation, in which the auditor tries to ascertain the speaker's single meaning, and literature, where the element of play is so strong that readers may impose whatever readings they please.

Whereas STRUCTURALISM has its foundations in linguistics and anthropology, deconstruction, sometimes called poststructuralism, is grounded in philosophy. Deconstruction has its roots in the assaults of Nietzsche, Freud, and Heidegger on the prevailing metaphysics and the denial of the possibility of discovering truth. As critic, the deconstructionist wants to "subvert without pity the obvious and stubborn referentiality behind a word or figure," says Leitch, a new intention in criticism that gives rise to new critical forms. Virtually without exception, deconstructive criticism eschews the styleless style, the brick-on-brick mode of conventional critical writing, and is instead playful, subjective, allusive, epigrammatic. (Walter Kendrick says that Derrida's *Glas* combines "literature, philosophy, autobiography, and a heavy dose of Space Invaders.") Leitch's essay "The Book of Deconstructive Criticism" has chapters interspersed with notes, commentaries, and advertisements; it ends with a review of itself (largely negative) a letter of response to the review, and an afterword. Deconstructionists are fond of such neologisms as "difference," which acknowledges that a word on a page denominates a simultaneous presence/absence: "apple" suggests the fruit to a hungry reader as much as it reminds him or her that there is no fruit to be had, only ink on paper.

Leitch maintains that "all texts can be deconstructed: all texts can be shown to be at once referential and fictive and at the same time to be based on the play of absence and presence." While this may be true, certainly some texts offer themselves for deconstruction more readily than others. Italo Calvino's *If on a Winter's Night a Traveler* begins as itself and then becomes Tazio Bazakbal's *Outside the Town of Malbork*, which in turn becomes

Ukko Ahti's *Leaning from the Steep Slope*, undergoing transformation after transformation until the reader wants to throw the book "out of the closed window, through the slats of the Venetian blinds; let them shred its incongruous quires, let sentences, words, morphemes, phonemes gush forth, beyond recomposition . . . let it be degraded into a swirling entropy." This is a chicken-or-egg issue, of course, and rather than say that the literature is written for the criticism or vice versa, perhaps it would be better to consider them parallel expressions of a single post-Nietzschean (Freudian/Heideggerian) viewpoint.

And regardless of one's stance on these matters, it is necessary to recognize the problems that arise if, as Robert Langbaum says, the goal of deconstructive analysis is to open "as many entries into the text as possible while resisting the establishment of a center of final coherence." To return to Derrida's distinction between conversation and literature, is criticism not conversation? If it is not, then to read a critic like Harold Bloom, complains Walter Kendricks, is "a vertiginous, invigorating experience, but it is doubtful that it "teaches you anything—except how to cavort with the mind of Harold Bloom." (No strict deconstructionist himself, Bloom is a self-styled "misreader" whose method is nonetheless often associated with that of Derrida and others.) Too, since no critical activity can occur outside of academe and its master-apprentice hierarchy, one must concern oneself with the larger implications of any critical cabala. Frederick Crews issues this warning: "In now declaring that there are no standards of evidence, no intentions worth deciphering, nothing but more or less creative misreadings, these same spokesmen are anticipating a day when there would be only one access route to the inner sanctum. It would be the path of currying favor with *them*—imitating their mannerisms, praising their cleverness, using their favorite code words from the latest Parisian sources." Vico warned centuries ago that the rulers keep the gods to themselves, which may be good religion, though it is certainly bad government. Besides, everyone wants to be a ruler. Kendricks echoes Crews's admonition when he notes that "home-grown structuralists" used to glut academic journals and conferences; today they've been replaced by flat-footed deconstructors à la Derrida and weak misreaders who strain to seem as strong as Bloom."

Those who want to deconstruct deconstruction seem more concerned about such effects as these than they are about the major spokesmen themselves, whose work they view with a genuine, albeit grudging, admiration; they neither blame Bloom nor deride Derrida. No doubt the antideconstructionists can sympathize with Isaac Bashevis Singer's feelings on genius. Singer is reputed to have said, "One Kafka in a century is wonderful. Two would be a disaster."

**Delphi technique**   A forecasting technique developed by the Rand Corporation in which expert opinion is solicited through a series of four questionnaires, each a refined version of the previous one. Presuming a high degree of expertise on the part of those polled, the Delphi technique relies on anonymity (so that no one can be swayed be a forceful but misinformed arguer, as on a committee) and a statistical response (in which everyone's opinion, not just that of the majority, is used in the refinement of the projections that go into each successive questionnaire). An example would be an attempt at predicting when half of the power plants in a given country would be nuclear; as each questionnaire included more and more information from the various experts—about the current state of technology, the population's attitudes toward nuclear power, and so on—presumably a reliable projection would be reached in short order. Marvin J. Cetron characterizes the Delphi technique as "an elegant method for developing a consensus."

**determinism**   The belief that every event has a cause; in human terms, the denial of free will. NATURALISM is a deterministic viewpoint, in which heredity and environment alone shape human behavior.

**dialectical materialism**   Formulated by Friedrich Engels, who never actually used the phrase himself, and applied to social and historical events by Karl Marx, dialectical materialism is the belief that progress occurs only through struggle between economic classes. It derives from Georg Wilhelm Friedrich Hegel's dialectical logic, originally a method of inquiry that argued that a concept or thesis will generate its opposite or antithesis and interact with it to form a new concept or synthesis (which in turn becomes the thesis of a new sequence).

**dialectical method**   See ZENO'S PARADOXES.

**dichotomy**   The division of something into two opposed parts, e.g., the division of the universe into mind and matter.

**diminishing returns, law of**   Also called the law of decreasing returns and the law of variable proportions, this economic law states that if one factor in production (labor, goods, capital) is increased without increasing the others, returns will decrease relative to what they were previously. The law of diminishing returns is attributed to British economist David Ricardo, even though it was anticipated by other thinkers.

**displacement**   In physics, the replacement of one mass by another, as in the displacement of a volume of fluid by a submerged body; in psychoanalysis, the shifting of an emotion or attitude to someone other than the one who originally aroused it, as when you are angry at your father but hit your younger brother because your father is bigger than you are.

Displacement has an economic meaning as well. In *Supermoney* Adam Smith says that it means "the framework will be the same, but inside you move things." Smith then reports a discussion of automobile stocks with one rather cynical investor. "I told him that one problem among others in certain localities was dope addiction, and at one plant—though the number sounded very high to me—the rate was reported to be 14 percent.

'Well,' he said, 'I haven't owned an auto stock for years. But fourteen percent! Geez, *who makes the needles?*' "

**dissociation of sensibility**   A sundering of thought and feeling. In his 1921 essay "The Metaphysical Poets," T.S. Eliot praised John Donne and his successors for mingling thought and feeling in their poetry. On the other hand, Milton and Dryden were guilty of a "dissociation of sensibility" from ideas in their poetry and had passed this legacy down to such nineteenth-century poets as Tennyson and Browning.

**dissociative reaction**   A reaction to events one causes but does not remember. An extreme case is the so-called Hillside Strangler, who killed a number of young women on the West Coast in the 1970s. Whereas normal children often have imaginary playmates who disappear as the child grows older, some children develop totally alternative personalities; a "good" child with overly strict parents may develop a "bad" playmate who alone is responsible for any improper actions on the child's part. The Strangler, a polite and sensitive man whose real name was Ken Bianchi, would sometimes find himself walking along a road, not remembering how he got there or why he had gone; as detailed in Ted Schwarz's account, it was during these dissociative periods that the murders were committed by "Steve," Ken's profane and murderous alter ego.

**divergent infinite series**   See INFINITE SERIES.

**Doppler effect**   See RED SHIFT.

**double helix**   This phrase describes the structure of the DNA (deoxyribonucleic acid) molecule, the fundamental genetic material present in the chromosomes of all cells. The book *The Double Helix*, by Nobel laureate James D. Watson, describes his discovery of this structure in 1953 in collaboration with Francis Crick and is considered a classic description of the errors, the rivalries, the crushing disappointments, and the heady successes of modern team science.

**dualism**  Any philosophical system that explains all phenomena in terms of two distinct principles, such as mind and matter or good and evil; the opposite of MONISM. Typically, dualists are interested in the Other: something they want to attract (money, the opposite sex) or repel (cancer, foreign ideologies). The dualist is active, moralistic, aggressive, involved, as opposed to the monist, who is quietistic, contemplative, passive, detached.

**duration**  Clock time is a medium in which things are arranged one after another, as in space. But according to Henri Bergson, real or mental time or, as he called it, duration (*la durée*), is a qualitative rather than a quantitative state; it is not divisible or measurable and in it ideas, memories, and feelings may interpenetrate. See STREAM OF CONSCIOUSNESS.

# E

**ego**   The part of the mind that reacts to the external world, handling its demands as it mediates between the primitive impulses of the ID and the stern urgings of the SUPEREGO.

**élan vital**   The life force in nature that is expressed through evolution; a form of VITALISM. The phrase is from Henri Bergson, who saw this force as a nonverifiable, intuitively grasped flow of consciousness through nature and the universe.

**empiricism**   The theory that all knowledge derives from experience; the opposite of APRIORISM. Most modern physicists are empiricists, seeking only to describe their observations with accuracy rather than attempting to define an underlying "reality" (see QUANTUM MECHANICS for an elaboration). See also INDUCTION and POSITIVISM.

**entelechy**   In Aristotle's philosophy, a thing's realization as opposed to its potentiality; also the vital principle in something that leads to its realization. A form of VITALISM.

**entropy**   See THERMODYNAMICS, LAWS OF, and MAXWELL'S DEMON.

**Epimenides' paradox**   Epimenides was a Cretan who said, "All Cretans are liars." So was he telling the truth or not? Also called the liar paradox, this paradox may be stated even more simply by saying, "I am lying" or "This is a false statement."

**epiphenomenon**   See HIDDEN-VARIABLE THEORY.

**epistemology**   The study of knowledge: its sources, its varieties, its limits. See APRIORISM and EMPIRICISM.

**eschatology**   A concern with the end of the world. In philosophy and science, the emphasis would be on the final moment of time; in theology, on the Day of Judgment, the future state of the soul, and so on.

**event horizon**   A turning point, an outermost limit; in a collapsing star, the point at which light stops and begins to turn back on itself. Thus the region around a BLACK HOLE would be defined by its event horizon.

William J. Kaufmann III says that the term "event horizon" is appropriate because "it is literally a *horizon* in the geometry of space and time beyond which you cannot see any *events*. You have no way of knowing what is happening inside an event horizon. You cannot communicate with anyone on the other side of an event horizon. It is a place disconnected from our space and time. It is not part of our universe."

**evolution**   The gradual development of life forms in accordance with the principle of NATURAL SELECTION. See also QUANTUM SPECIATION.

**excluded middle, law of**   This classic law of logic argues that every proposition is either true or false; there is no middle ground. Such scientific principles as COMPLEMENTARITY have suggested that the law of the excluded middle no longer holds in every case.

**existentialism**   Though there are different and even conflicting "existentialisms," in general this philosophical movement,
which has its roots in the writings of Søren Kierkegaard and was
developed by Martin Heidegger and Jean Paul Sartre (among others), emphasizes the exercise of the will in the face of a hostile universe. According to Philip P. Hallie, the existentialist is opposed
to "the secular and religious laws or abstractions that make a man
not a passionately *deciding*, spiritual being, but a passionlessly
*conforming*, cog-like being, incapable of deep feeling, incapable of
his own spiritual or moral choices." Many writers find existentialism particularly applicable to the twentieth century because it offers an answer to madness that has never before operated on a
global scale. Prompted by Hitler, Mussolini, economic depression,
and the dehumanizing effects of industrialization, the individual
set out on an "independent, often anti-ideological search for
value," says Christopher Butler, an essentially existential search
that "provided a sense of purpose which was necessary for recov-
ery from the fascist period, and gave confidence to the avant-
garde." See HUMANISTIC PSYCHOLOGY.


**expectation-fit ratio**   In perceptual terms, what is expected usually fits: fire burns, an object falls when dropped, and
so on. A weak expectation-fit ratio means accident or surprise and
is therefore at the heart of much literature and almost all humor; a
Connecticut Yankee is knocked unconscious and wakes up in King
Arthur's court. But most discoveries involve less elaborate circumstances. The trick is for scientists, artists, or historians to
block out information not critical to their activity (otherwise they
would be paralyzed by every minute occurrence) yet perceive the
richness and complexity that is ordinarily blocked by those with
other concerns or more modest gifts. The narrator of the greatest
Dutch novel of the nineteenth century, *Max Havelaar*, by
"Multatuli" (Edward Douwes Dekker), says: "I can imagine that
to witness, or even to participate in, important events may make
little or no impact on a certain type of disposition which has not the
capacity for receiving and absorbing impressions. If anyone
doubts this, let him ask himself whether he would be justified in

crediting with 'experience' all the inhabitants of France who were forty or fifty years old in 1815. And yet all of these were persons who had not only seen the stupendous drama that began with 1789 but had even played in it, some more or less important role." Thus the greatest authority on a particular conflict may be the scholar who has sifted impartially through various reports and not the actual combatant whose strong expectation-fit ratio permitted him or her to see only what was expected (a "deficiency" that no doubt guaranteed survival on the battlefield, a bad place for impartiality). In America the history of the post–Civil War South is marred by distorted accounts; Avery Craven writes that "a number of observers went South to inspect and report on conditions. Historians as a rule are very skeptical of travelers, who, they know, take prejudices with them on their journeys and find largely what they want to find."

Perhaps for this reason, a weak expectation-fit ratio is the *sine qua non* of serious literature. Literature is less a matter of creation than of observation, and of a certain kind; Melville's ideal is Ishmael, who celebrates the complexity of the ordinary world, not Ahab with his destructive tunnel vision. "I am become a transparent eyeball," says Emerson, "I am nothing; I see all." "We are as much as we see," according to Thoreau. Whitman asks himself, "What do you see Walt Whitman?" in his poem "Salut au Monde" and answers himself eighty-three times, beginning each time with the words "I see. . . ." When asked in 1929 what he liked best about himself, William Carlos Williams replied, "My ability to be drunk with a sudden realization of value in things others never notice." And recently William Burroughs said, "Most people don't see what's going on around them. That's my principal message to writers: For Godsake, keep your *eyes* open."


**experience, law of**    First suggested in the 1950s by British engineer W. Ross Ashby, this law says that new information destroys old information of a similar nature. Flo Conway and Jim Siegelman give the example of a rider who falls off her horse and is urged to remount quickly; her negative experience must be replaced with a positive one if she is to overcome the trauma of the fall and continue to make progress with her horsemanship. The law of experience has obvious implications for the fields of CYBERNETICS and INFORMATION THEORY.

**expressionism**   An artistic mode that seeks to express mental states, often neurotic and distorted ones, rather than an objective external reality. Edvard Munch and Vincent Van Gogh are often mentioned as forefathers of expressionism, which characterizes the paintings of Georges Rouault and Oskar Kokoschka, the fiction of Franz Kafka, and such films as Robert Weine's *The Cabinet of Dr. Caligari* (1920) and Fritz Lang's *M* (1933). See ULTRAISM.

# F

**feedback**    The casual use of "feedback" to mean "response" is anathema to students of CYBERNETICS, since feedback is a form of automatic self-regulation by which part of the output of an electrical, mechanical, or biological system is returned as input. Similarly, "negative feedback" does not mean "criticism." Negative feedback is actually a virtue in a system because it indicates that the system is overextending itself; if an engine starts to go too fast, negative feedback is what impels a valve to reduce automatically the supply of fuel and thus reduce the engine's speed to a predetermined level of maximum efficiency. The reverse of such a self-limiting situation and an example of positive feedback would be a profitable economic system that, while distributing most of its profits in the form of salaries, services, and so on, retains at least part of its gain and uses it to expand the system itself, thereby ensuring increased profits and indefinite growth. The first example shows how negative feedback has a benevolent and stabilizing effect, since the idea is to keep the engine running at the same speed all the time. The second example shows how positive feedback has a destabilizing effect (in this case, also benevolent), since the intent this time is to cause the situation to change constantly.

**fetishism**    A sexual abnormality in which pleasure is fixed on an object, such as a shoe, a fur, or a whip. Fetishism is frequently associated with MASOCHISM, since the fetishist willingly subjugates himself to an object of no great importance, thus making

himself even less significant. Most fetishists are male; psychoanalysts believe that the fetish is a substutute for the male genitals
and that it "completes" the female for men who otherwise think of
women as deprived.

**Fibonacci sequence**   The sequence 0, 1, 1, 2, 3, 5, 8, 13,
21, 34, and so on—in other words, each new value is the sum of the
two values immediately preceding it. The Fibonacci sequence has
a variety of applications in higher mathematics and was propounded around the year 1202 by Leonardo of Pisa, son of
Bonaccio, thus "filius Bonacci " or Fibonacci. Leonardo was also
an early advocate of the use of Arabic rather than Roman
numerals.

**field physics**   See GESTALT.

**foreshortening**   In art, to represent objects as diminished
in such a way as to comply with the laws of PERSPECTIVE; the
technique by which the artist places all objects in correct proportion to all other objects in a drawing or painting and causes them
to seem of the relative proper size.

What is assumed is that one's line of vision is roughly parallel to
the objects viewed. Angles alter the laws of perspective; when F.
Scott Fitzgerald complained to Hemingway about the inadequate
size of his sexual member, Hemingway replied, "You look at yourself from above and you look foreshortened."

**formalism**   An analytical method that emphasized style and
structure in art, formalism flourished in Russia in the 1920s, finding a natural ally in CONSTRUCTIVISM. As with that movement, however, formalism fell into disfavor with the rise of SO-
CIALIST REALISM, which concerned itself almost entirely with
the subject matter of art and denigrated the importance of form,
especially in modern or "decadent" art. See MINIMALISM.

**free association**   See CATHARSIS.


**futurism**   A movement in the arts in Italy that came to have international implications, futurism began with the 1909 manifesto of poet Filippo Tommaso Marinetti, who, along with other writers, painters, and sculptors, glorified the fruits of the Industrial Revolution: danger, war, speed, machines. This emphasis on the heady dynamism of contemporary life as opposed to the stodgy past led to a natural if informal alliance between futurism and other movements in the arts, such as CONSTRUCTIVISM, CUBISM, and DADA; by the same token, the futurists contributed indirectly to the rise of Fascism in Italy. In music, futurism took the form of *bruitisme* (French "noisiness"), which was based on industrial sounds. See ART DECO and CUBO-FUTURISM.

# G

**galaxy**   One of billions of systems of billions of stars (as well as gas and dust) that make up the UNIVERSE; about a million galaxies are within the range of the earth's largest telescopes. The earth itself belongs to a SOLAR SYSTEM located about halfway from the center of the galaxy called the Milky Way.

**game theory**   Mathematician John Von Neumann, whose work contributed to the QUANTUM THEORY and the development of the atomic bomb, is the chief founder of game theory. This branch of mathematics deals with the choices available to participants in situations that involve conflicts of interest. One of Von Neumann's early games was the zero-sum game, in which the total gain (and loss) of the participants is always zero; thus a card game is always a zero-sum game unless the house takes a cut of the winnings. Von Neumann's mathematical techniques for keeping gains as high and losses as low as possible are more useful insofar as they clarify the nature of the problem of choice than as surefire guarantees of success. As Rudolf Peierls notes, game theory "has not yet led any gambler into making a fortune, because in practice the job of enumerating all the strategies that may arise from any strategy of the opponent is prohibitive except in the simplest examples, such as a game of tick-tack-toe on a small field."

Von Neumann's terms have widespread use; a book by Lester Thurow, for example, is called *The Zero-Sum Society* (one in which growth is stalled, thus making one group's gain another's loss). With its idea of establishing coalitions between participants to maximize gain or minimize loss, game theory is particularly applicable to politics and to war. When the conduct of such endeavors seems less than reasonable, it is amusing to consider the name Von Neumann gave to the computer that enabled the United States to produce the first hydrogen bomb. It was called MANI-AC, an acronym for *m*athematical *a*nalyzer, *n*umerical *i*ntegrator, *a*nd *c*omputer.

**Ganser syndrome**   Also known as the syndrome of approximate answers, this phenomenon (as described by psychologist S. J. M. Ganser) is seen in the attempt of criminals to feign mental illness by giving silly approximate answers to questions. ("When were you born?" "Last year.") An impression of mental illness may be given to the lay observer, but specialists are supposedly able to recognize the deception.

A disturbing possibility, however, and one that suggests the fragility of the human psyche, is the development of Ganser syndrome into real insanity. In *The Making of a Counter Culture*, Theodore Roszak says that "the syndrome describes the behavior of people who seem to be faking insanity, but faking it so well that they eventually take on their insane role permanently. In a sense, they calculatedly drive themselves mad." To novelist Mary McCarthy, "Feigning is a perilous business; the actor loses himself or, worse, finds himself in the part he assumes."

**Gaussian distribution**   Also called the normal distribution, the Gaussian distribution is seen in the celebrated bell-shaped curve formed by school test results, with the greatest number of grades being average and the number of excellent and poor grades being approximately equal; named for Karl Friedrich Gauss, commonly ranked with Newton as one of the greatest mathematicians of all time. See POISSON DISTRIBUTION and PROBABILITY THEORY.

**Gedanken experiment**   An experiment performed only

in the mind (from German *Gedanke*, "thought"). In *A Comprehensible World*, Jeremy Bernstein observes that a great *Gedanken* experiment always leads to a new scientific PARADIGM. He gives the example of the sixteen-year-old Albert Einstein wondering if he could see himself in a mirror were both he and it moving at the speed of light. Einstein realized that he could not solve the problem in terms of classical physics, and further thought led him to the formulation of the special theory of RELATIVITY.

**Gestalt**   Literally German "form." Gestalt thinking in the arts as well as the sciences means that a given whole has properties not derivable from any of its individual parts or their mechanical sum. In psychology, the Gestalt school was given impetus by Max Wertheimer, who, along with his colleagues, protested the prevailing atomistic trend in psychology and attempted to view the workings of the mind macroscopically rather than microscopically. Other examples of Gestalt thinking can be seen in field physics, in which the bodies of a region are studied in terms of their gravitational, electromagnetic, or nuclear interaction with other bodies, and IMPRESSIONISM, whereby splashes of paint that are meaningless when examined closely form a harmonious whole when viewed from the proper distance. See also HOLISM and PERSISTENCE OF VISION.

**Gödel's theorem**   In 1931 mathematician and logician Kurt Gödel became what Gerald Jonas calls "one of the spoilsports of modern science." His theorem shows that every branch of mathematics is based on propositions that cannot be proved within the system itself and that therefore no system is either complete or self-sufficient. Reconciling Gödel with modern literature, Douglas Fowler notes (in *A Reader's Guide to Gravity's Rainbow*) that his theorem guarantees that there will always be "paradoxes, inexplicabilities, new events, and dark corners"—bad news for the logical positivist, perhaps, but "good news for the artist."

Once again a barrier to human inquiry seems to have been revealed. In his *Critique of Practical Reason* (1788), Kant proposed that there were limits to the mind's abilities; in *Irrational Man*,

William Barrett says that "science has in this century, with the discoveries of Heisenberg in physics and Gödel in mathematics, at last caught up with Kant." See UNCERTAINTY PRINCIPLE.

**gnosticism**  The Greek word *gnosis* means "knowledge," and gnostics claim to have privileged insight into spiritual matters; by definition, then, they are always at odds with the authorities. Historically, the gnostics were a heretical Christian sect whose pronouncements were murky and unsystematic. ("Every day everyone of them invents something new," complained the church father Irenaeus.) Nowadays gnosticism is extended to HERMETIC beliefs of all kinds, from cult movements to pop versions of Jungian psychology.

**googol**  The largest number: one followed by a hundred zeroes. The word was adopted by American mathematician Edward Kasner from a child's nonsense word for any enormous number. If asked, "Why not simply add a hundred and one zeroes?," one might reply, "Because one has to draw the line somewhere." Or, as William Blake said, "Truth has limits, Error none."

In fact, according to Kasner, there *is* a larger number: the googolplex, which is one with a googol zeroes behind it.

**great numbers, law of**  See PROBABILITY THEORY.

**Gresham's law**  This law says that bad money drives out good. Associated with sixteenth-century English merchant and financier Sir Thomas Gresham, this economic principle apparently predated its reputed author and in fact was never stated by him in any way. Regardless of its origins, the idea is that debased coinage will be allowed to stay in circulation indefinitely, whereas coins whose value as precious metal exceeds their value as money will be driven out of circulation and hoarded.

Generally, Gresham's law can be taken to mean simply that the bad will always be victorious. In his short story "Otto and the

Magi," Evan S. Connell demonstrates the adaptability of this economic principle. The main character, Muhlbach, exhausts himself by his attempts to communicate with his secretive son, Otto. The boy has acquired a pedometer, and Muhlbach wants to know how it has worked. "But the answer, customarily, was Otto's favorite; that is, he didn't know, wasn't sure, or had forgotten how far he had gone that day. Then of what use is a pedometer, if you don't know, or already have forgotten? Well, having thought this over, of course, he didn't know. Victory belongs to the ignorant, a variation of Gresham's law."

# H

**habitat theory**   See PROSPECT-REFUGE theory.

**Hawthorne effect**   Experiments conducted between 1924 and 1936 in the Hawthorne plant of the Western Electric Company (near Chicago) showed that productivity increased following any new policy change by management that the workers interpreted as benevolent, regardless of the specific incentives involved. Thus it is the seeming good intent behind change that results in improved performance, not the change itself.

**hegemony**   Originally meaning the dominance of one state over others, as in the British hegemony during the heyday of the Empire, the term has been used by Italian Marxist Antonio Gramsci and others to mean class dominance, as in the bourgeois hegemony. In this sense, hegemony refers to more than military might and connotes the pervasiveness of a class consciousness with its attendant aspirations, prejudices, and social certainties.

**hermeneutics**   Originally the art of interpretation as applied to the Bible, hermeneutics now means interpretation in general and is used particularly by those who see interpretation as a science.

**hermetic**   The Egyptian god Thoth, supposed founder of the occult sciences, was called Hermes Trismegistus by the Greeks; from this name comes the word hermetic, suggesting the occult or magic in general.

The term has a specialized application as well: in the 1920s and 30s, a movement in Italian poetry developed called *la poesia ermetica*, which advocated the elimination of rhetoric and emphasized the importance of pure diction made resonant by blankness and silence. Important figures in the movement included Giuseppe Ungaretti and, later, Eugenio Montale and Salvatore Quasimodo. W.S. Di Piero notes that the goals of this group were "a new kind of anti-eloquence, of mineral understatement . . . ecstasy in intimate commonplaces, and a language of brilliant privacy."

**Hertzsprung-Russell diagram**   See STELLAR EVOLUTION.

**heuristic**   A method or model that stimulates the student to carry out his or her own investigation. Often a discovery that becomes invalid retains some significance as a heuristic; thus Michael H. Hart notes that "Bohr's picture of the atom is of great heuristic value, even though modern scientists do not consider it literally correct."

**hidden-variable theory**   According to David Bohm, there is a subquantum world of hidden variables, one that underlies the quantum level of reality and from which that reality emerges. In other words, the space-time world of quantum physics is an epiphenomenon (i.e., one phenomenon caused by another). Bohm uses this dependence of the quantum world on hidden variables to explain the seeming acausality of QUANTUM MECHANICS.

**Hilbert's problems**   David Hilbert was a German mathematician and philosopher; the *Mathematics Dictionary* calls

him simply the "leading mathematician of the twentieth century."
In 1900 he presented a paper entitled "Mathematical Problems" to
the Second International Congress of Mathematics in Paris.
Hilbert's list of twenty-three problems has, writes Jeremy
Bernstein in *The New Yorker*, "all but defined mathematics for
much of this century"; further, "most of the problems have opened
up entirely new fields of mathematics." Little wonder that a colleague of his is reported to have said of Hilbert's work, "This is not
mathematics, this is theology."

A German in France speaking the international language of
mathematics in the first year of the new century: what better metaphor for the dawn of the Age of Science, with its attendant
themes of progress and cooperation? Unhappily, that Germany
and France were shortly at each other's throats in a war that
changed civilization forever suggests that mere knowledge is never enough.

**historical criticism**   The examination of an artwork in
terms of how it reflects both the period it was written in and its
author's life. The NEW CRITICISM came about largely as an antidote to historical criticism.

**holism**   The belief that wholes are more than the sums of their
parts and cannot be explained in terms of the properties of those
parts and their relation to each other; a synonym for organicism.
Physicist John Albright says no one can deny holism who has seen
a cat stalk a bird. If the cat were to approach the problem bit by
bit, cats would have dropped out of the evolutionary chain long
ago. In *Zen in the Art of Archery*, Eugen Herrigel emphasizes the
error of too much concentration on hitting the target; the Japanese masters under whom Herrigel studied believed that the
archer and the target, like the cat and the bird, are not two
opposing objects but one reality.

While not an argument against thought *per se*, the concept of
holism does argue against too much thought at the wrong time, on
the part of an athlete trying to kick a ball through a goal, for example, or a dancer who wants to perform a tricky step in time with

others; choreographer George Balanchine said that dancers should not think but do. See GESTALT.

**holography**   A form of three-dimensional photography based on laser use. The light waves are recorded on a plate called a hologram in such a way that waves from all parts of the object photographed are recorded on all parts of the hologram; thus the entire image may be reproduced from any part of the hologram, no matter how small.

Some neurophysiologists have argued the hologrammatic nature of the brain, saying that every part includes the whole. This is why a religious conversion, for example, may not only alter specific beliefs but change one's entire personality. In their study of sudden personality change among converts to American cult movements, Flo Conway and Jim Siegelman note that "the sudden injection of experience may destroy some specific pattern of thought, feeling, or belief, but it may also alter the entire focus of consciousness, shifting the window of individual awareness or changing the landscape altogether."

**Hubble's law**   Around 1928, Edwin Powell Hubble undertook the measurement of the universe. He found that even the nearest galaxies were millions of light years away; as Robert Jastrow says, "A few people had guessed that the Universe was large, but until Hubble made his measurements, no one knew how big a place it really is." Along the way, Hubble formulated the law that takes his name and is also known as the law of the expanding universe; it says that the farther away a galaxy is, the faster it moves.

Jastrow explains Hubble's law by means of a simple analogy. Suppose you were sitting in a lecture hall that suddenly doubled in size. Your immediate neighbor, who had been three feet away, is now six feet away. But a person on the other side of the hall who had been 300 feet distant from you, is now 600 feet away. Clearly that person moved at a faster speed. All uniformly expanding objects, including balloons and rising loaves of bread, are subject to

Hubble's law; if their outer surfaces moved at the same speed as their insides they would begin to compress after a time rather than expand. See BIG-BANG THEORY and RED SHIFT.

**humanism**  The belief in the importance of human aspirations and achievements. Often associated with the rise of CLASSICISM during the Renaissance, humanism breaks with the medieval tradition of subordinating the human to the divine.

**humanistic psychology**  A school associated mainly with Abraham Maslow, humanistic psychology is informed by EXISTENTIALISM and promotes consciousness, awareness, and self-actualization. It is opposed to the Freudian school, which sees the individual as controlled by secret inner voices, as well as BEHAVIORISM, which emphasizes the external forces that shape lives; each of these schools subscribes to what the humanistic psychologists describe as a limited "robot man" model of behavior. In turn, psychologists from the Freudian and behavioral schools criticize the humanists for their impossible promise of a heightened reality for everyone.

**hysteria**  A type of NEUROSIS marked by emotional excitability well as visual sensory and motor disturbances. In a paper entitled "On Hysteria," Freud writes that "every hysteria is founded in repression, always with a sexual content," and in "Some Neurotic Mechanisms in Jealousy, Paranoia and Homosexuality" he elaborates, noting that "the pathogenic phantasies, derivatives of repressed instinctual impulses, are for a long time tolerated alongside the normal life of the mind, and have no pathogenic effect until by a revolution in the libidinal economy they receive a hypercathexis; not till then does the conflict which leads to the formation of symptoms break out." The classic illustration of this development is the story of Anna O.; see TRANSFERENCE. See also CATHEXIS and LIBIDO.

# I

**id**   The unconscious and primitive part of the mind dominated by the PLEASURE PRINCIPLE. See also EGO and SUPEREGO.

**idealism**   The theory that says that everything exists only in the mind; the opposite of MATERIALISM. The eighteenth-century divine Bishop Berkeley is among the best-known idealist philosophers; his maxim *esse est percipi* (to be is to be perceived) states plainly the basic premise of idealism.

When told by Boswell of Berkeley's seemingly irrefutable thesis, Dr. Johnson kicked a stone that was in his path, saying, "I refute it *thus*." Of course an idealist would maintain that the rock, the kick, and the subsequent pain to the great man's foot, however palpable they may have seemed, were all purely mental phenomena. See ONTOLOGY.

**image**   See SYMBOL.

**imagism**   Like many movements in the arts that developed during the early days of MODERNISM, imagism arose as a revolt against the pretentious, the inflated, the conventional. The imagist poet strives for absolute clarity; perhaps the best-known poem of the school is William Carlos Williams's "The Red Wheelbarrow" (1923), with its short lines, simple images, and seeming absence of message. Denis Donoghue says that "Imagism is the Minimalism of poetry; its prescriptions are: no this, no that, no ideas, no comments, no adjectives, write the poem as if you were carving a piece of wood, cut away the excess, leave only the tensions and the rhythms." Ezra Pound was one of the founders of the group, and his affinity for Oriental poetry and particularly the Japanese haiku is reflected in the aims of imagism.

Another characteristic that imagism shared with other artistic movements of the early twentieth century (such as DADA) was an emphasis on flamboyant public-relations efforts. The outspoken, cigar-smoking, and often profane Amy Lowell effectively took over the imagist movement from Pound and touted it through a series of public readings and anthologies. Pound renamed the movement "Amygism." See also ACMEISM.


**impressionism**   A school of painting that began in France in the late nineteenth century and went on to affect not only the visual arts in the twentieth century but music and literature as well. Characterized by the attempt to capture transitory impressions of light and color with bright splashes of paint, impressionist painting opposes the anecdotal nature of traditional art as well as conventional choices of subject matter—indeed, it is a reaction against the dictates of the official art world, and Roger Shattuck notes that impressionism is "the first artistic movement entirely organized in cafés." The name was coined by a hostile journalist and comes from a painting by Claude Monet entitled *Impression—Soleil Levant* ("Impression—Sunrise") that was included in the first impressionist exhibition in 1874, a show organized by disgruntled artists whose works had been rejected by the Salon, the annual juried art show presented by the French Academy.

Similarly, musical impressionism throws off the yoke of heavily dominant rhythms and harmonies and substitutes description and color for the romantic dynamism of such composers as Beethoven. Its best-known exponent is Claude Debussy, whose tone poem *Prélude à l'Après-midi d'un Faune* relies on the whole-tone scale instead of the traditional scale, thus producing a deliberately nebulous and dreamy effect.

Literary impressionism, though more difficult to define than either the artistic or musical variety, nonetheless conveys with greater authority the impressionist's intent to capture, not reality itself, but the effect of reality on the viewer. Accordingly, literary impressionism has a discontinuous, evocative, unfinished quality to it. The STREAM OF CONSCIOUSNESS technique is an example of literary impressionism, and Virginia Woolf is a representative literary impressionist.

***induction***   Reasoning from the particular to the general; using numerous instances of a given phenomenon in order to establish a principle—if most of the rats injected with an experimental substance die, for example, then that substance is probably lethal.

Induction is the scientific method of inference (see EMPIRICISM), which is to say that it is the uncertain method. If DEDUCTION leads to specific and inescapable inferences, induction leads to what Warren Weaver describes as "judgments concerning the plausibility of various general conclusions" (what is lethal to rats, after all, may be neutral or benign to other species). As the scientific method, inductive reasoning did not achieve its real importance until late in the eighteenth century. After deduction, says Weaver, induction is the second great stage of intellectual liberation. See also BAYES'S THEOREM; Francis Bacon was the first proponent of induction as a scientific method, but Bayes made induction truly useful by giving it a mathematical basis.

***infinite series***   In mathematics, a series of numbers that goes on forever. There are three kinds: convergent infinite series, which approach finitude (1/2 + 1/4 + 1/8 + 1/16, etc.); divergent infinite series, which approach infinitude (1 + 2 + 3 + 4, etc.); and oscillating infinite series, which approach no number (1 + 1 − 1 + 1, etc.).

***inflationary universe***   According to the inflationary

model of the universe, originated in 1980 by particle theorist Alan H. Guth of the Massachusetts Institute of Technology, the universe developed from a concentration of energy that may have been smaller than an atomic particle. This model says that particles began to form on the subatomic level, then combine and disappear into new combinations almost instantly; the recombinations occurred so quickly as to sidestep the CONSERVATION LAWS and produce the entire universe from virtually nothing.

To many scientists, the inflationary model explains better than the BIG-BANG THEORY such anomalies as the uniformity of elements throughout the universe, the uniform and smooth expansion of the universe, and the fortuitous rate of expansion (neither so quickly that galaxies would fail to form nor so slowly that the universe might collapse upon itself). These observable truths are better explained, they say, by a model based on homogeneous and regular self-replication than one based on a fiery and turbulent explosion.

**information theory**   An outgrowth of CYBERNETICS, information theory not only deals with the transmission of information in technical systems but also concerns itself with the application of cybernetic principles to the human central nervous system. See also EXPERIENCE, LAW OF.

**intentional fallacy**   The mistake of judging a work of art in terms of its creator's stated intent. Wimsatt and Beardsley point out that a poem is "detached from the author at birth and goes about the world beyond his power to intend about it or control it"; thus whatever the poet says about the poem is "subject to the same scrutiny as any statement in linguistics or in the general science of psychology." After all, the poet may be half-concealing some shameful urge that prompted the poem or simply may not have grasped the splendor of the achievement. Poets, like everyone else, occasionally succeed in spite of themselves, and no one can be expected to know the contents of his or her unconscious

mind. Like the AFFECTIVE FALLACY, the intentional fallacy
is a tenet of the NEW CRITICISM in that it prompts a close look
at the whole text to the exclusion of all other matters.


***irony***   An ironic statement or event turns out to have the opposite of its perceived meaning. Paul Fussell maintains that irony
is the one form that dominates modern understanding and attributes this dominance to the impact on the public consciousness of
World War I, in which the lies of the press and the politicians
could not disguise the fact that warrior-heroes were simply frightened doughboys and the War to End All Wars was in reality the
first in a chain of progressively bloodier conflicts. Fussell deals at
length with one variety of irony that characterizes the literature
of modern warfare, namely, the stock scene in which a soldier
cares for a wounded comrade who is actually dying. An example is
in Joseph Heller's World War II novel *Catch-22* (1961), where
Yossarian comforts Snowden and discovers that his insides have
been shot out, even though Snowden, who does not realize that he
is dead (much less ironic), keeps complaining about the cold.

# J

**James-Lange theory**  Anyone who has ever started running to catch a bus, only to feel an inexplicable joy or terror or both, has proven the James-Lange theory. Taking C.G. Lange's belief that emotion results from changes in the cardiovascular system, William James argued in his *Principles of Psychology* (1890) that action precedes emotion. In the example given above, the runner feels what would be felt were he or she crossing a goal line or fleeing a dog, even though the situation calls for no such emotions.

In his own discussion of this theory, Jacques Barzun recalls Poe's story "The Purloined Letter," in which the narrator tells of a schoolboy who wins a guessing game called Odd or Even by imitating his opponents' facial expressions, the idea being that the assumption of each expression would lead to the feeling of the emotions that prompted it. Barzun goes on: "It is indeed the age-old advice of moralists and friendly comforters that we should 'go through the motions' of the feeling-state that is appropriate or desirable—dry the tears, erase the hangdog look and try to put on a cheerful face, hold up the head, keep a stiff upper lip, clench the jaw against fear, whistle in the dark as we would in sunshine—and with luck we shall feel the right emotion taking hold of us."

# L

**Lamarckism**  The theory of the inheritance of acquired characteristics as advocated by Jean Baptiste Antoine de Monet, Chevalier de Lamarck. The classic example is the long neck of the giraffe, which the giraffe supposedly acquired in order to browse among the leaves of trees. According to Darwinism, which refutes Lamarckism, the giraffe's neck developed spontaneously—the neck came first, then the trees, and not the other way around. Interestingly, Lamarckism helped prepare the way for Darwinism, since it does suggest gradual and continuous modifications of life forms over long periods of time.

Viewpoints that are apparently Lamarckist do surface from time to time, but usually due to misunderstandings. Susan West describes experiments by Reginald Gorczyniski and Edmund J. Steele in which male mice who had been made tolerant to foreign antigens passed that tolerance on to a large proportion of their offspring. Critics of the experiments referred to a "Lamarckist revival in immunology," though Gorczyniski and Steele maintain that the transfer of tolerance is actually made possible by a form of Darwinian selection that takes place at the cellular level. See LYSENKOISM.

**Le Châtelier's principle**  When a stable system is disturbed, the whole system will respond in such a way as to attempt to restore the original conditions. An example is the condensation of vapor that occurs when water is heated; the water becomes vapor, but the vapor returns to liquid form. This principle was enunciated by Henri Louis Le Châtelier, a French industrial chemist.

**liar paradox**   See EPIMENIDES' PARADOX.

**libido**   In early Freudian theory, libido meant only "sex drive," and those who misunderstand Freud, thinking him interested only in sex and nothing else, have retained that narrow meaning. In a later essay entitled "On Transience," however, Freud defines libido simply as the "capacity for love," and it is this meaning that is used consistently in Freud's mature work.

**life instinct**   See REPETITION COMPULSION.

**light year**   The distance light travels in one year, or about six trillion miles.

**local causes, principle of**   Since nothing can exceed the speed of light, according to the theory of RELATIVITY, causality must be "local," i.e., what is done at point A cannot affect what happens at point B if light from A cannot reach B until after what happens. See CAUSALITY, though.

**local color**   A subspecies of REALISM, local-color writing attempts to capture the speech, manners, customs, styles, attitudes, and prejudices of a particular region as it existed in the past; examples include the short stories and sketches of writers like Bret Harte, Joel Chandler Harris, and Sarah Orne Jewett.

According to Jay Martin, the local-colorist wants romantically to reconstruct the myth of the past or realistically destroy it or embody both tendencies because of a need "to reconstruct a glorious past, along with a simultaneous recognition that such a paradise never existed." This ambivalence is the main reason why local color is generally considered a second-rate literary school whose thematic limitations are transcended by the best authors. For example, William Faulkner is intensely Mississippian, but no one thinks of him as a local-colorist. Of course, Faulkner's works would not be the same were they set elsewhere, and thus he is sometimes described as an exponent of regionalism, as Thomas Hardy was in England. The difference is that a local-colorist is thematically limited to the realities of a time and place, whereas a regionalist deals in universal themes set against the backdrop of a specific locale.

*logology*   Literally, "words about words." Kenneth Burke coined this term to make it clear that his book *The Rhetoric of Religion* was not a theological study but a logological one, that is, one concerned only with the verbal forms of religious doctrines and the implications of these forms for an understanding of language in general.

*Lysenkoism*   Named for Trofim Denisovich Lysenko, this Russian form of LAMARCKISM dominated Soviet biology from the mid-1930s to 1965, when Lysenko was removed as director of the Institute of Genetics. During that period, many adherents to traditional theories of heredity were dismissed or liquidated. Like other theories of the Stalinist period, Lysenkoism was favored because of its emphasis on progress through manipulation of environment as opposed to the spontaneous development implicit in NATURAL SELECTION.

# M

**magic realism**    Located midway between the strict confines of REALISM and the boundless possibilities of SURREAL-
ISM, magic realism suggests a loosening of the ties of ordinary
life, not the complete abandonment of them. Recently associated
with the work of new South American fiction writers, magic realism characterizes a story by Julio Cortázar entitled "The Southern Thruway," in which a traffic jam outside Paris becomes a
semipermanent nation in which people are born, die, and so on.
Such a situation is at least possible, if not probable; by way of contrast, Eugene Ionesco's "Rhinoceros" is a surrealistic story because its characters actually turn into wild beasts. Magic realism
is represented in English by Tim O'Brien's *Going After Cacciato*,
in which an American Army deserter, fed up with the war in
Vietnam, walks the 8,600 miles from Saigon to Paris.


**Mannerism**    A late-sixteenth-century artistic style that emphasized technical proficiency, usually through detailed depiction
of the human figure in difficult and unusual poses. Mannerism has
its roots in the late work of Raphael and Michelangelo. Pontormo
and Parmagianino are representative Mannerist painters; in
sculpture, Mannerism reaches its peak in the works of Benvenuto
Cellini and Giambologna.


**masochism**    Specifically, an abnormality in which sexual
pleasure is derived from submission to physical abuse; generally,

an unconscious tendency to seek humiliation and defeat. The masochist wants to lose her- or himself and become an object. Thus masochism is the opposite of SADISM, which involves domination over others, and it is frequently associated with FETISHISM, in which one is dominated and humiliated by some insignificant object.

As is always the case with psychological opposites, however, masochism and sadism are often inseparable; Simone de Beauvoir reminds us that the Marquis de Sade had a favorite sadomasochistic fantasy in which he was being penetrated and beaten while he himself was penetrating and beating a third party.

Nor is there any particular reason always to see masochism as a function of the death instinct (see REPETITION-COMPULSION). The masochistic impulse can be self-protective. One such case involved a boy who would hoist up his rump to his father and receive a slap on the offending body part; the boy thought that by suffering this minor discomfort he could avoid castration at the father's hands, and since the annoyed parent slapped the boy at each of these rude demonstrations, a masochistic but (to the boy's mind) beneficial relationship was established.

Masochism takes its name from the Austrian novelist Leopold von Sacher-Masoch, author of *Venus in Furs* (1870) and other works that describe the pleasure of pain.


**materialism**   The theory that says that everything that is real can be experienced through the senses; the opposite of IDEALISM. Whereas a materialist in the popular sense is someone who wants a bigger car, a fancier house, and a better-looking mate than anyone else, a philosophical materialist is one who apprehends reality through rational, everyday senses. Thus Stoicism, Epicureanism, and Zen Buddhism are materialistic viewpoints because they are concerned with this world, whereas Platonism and Christianity are not because they posit a transcendent and "more real" reality (Plato's realm of ideas, the Christian heaven). See ONTOLOGY.


**mathematical logic**   See SYMBOLIC LOGIC.

**matrix**   See COMMUTATIVE MATHEMATICS.


**Maxwell's Demon**   Scottish physicist James Clerk Maxwell postulated a tiny demon who could produce perpetual motion,
thus denying the second law of THERMODYNAMICS. Max-
well's Demon sits in a box, sorting out fast air molecules from slow
ones and creating hot regions that can be used to drive an engine.
Thus a theoretician accuses another of "playing Maxwell's Demon" when suspecting him or her of falsely creating a system with
negative entropy, an impossibility.


**mechanism**   The theory that organisms are like machines in
that they are material systems governed by the laws of chemistry
and physics; the opposite of VITALISM. See also HOLISM.


**meliorism**   Generally, the belief that things will improve
(from the Latin *melior* "better"). Specifically, the Victorian belief
in an improving world that ended with World War I. Paul Fussell
calls this kind of meliorism "the Idea of Progress"; Martin
Seymour-Smith goes further and calls it "the myth of human progress." Seymour-Smith suggests that this myth was rooted in Victorian guilt about the technology that benefited the middle and
upper classes materially but that seemed to menace everyone's
spiritual lives, especially those of the masses of workers who
toiled twelve hours a day in the "dark Satanic mills" of which
Blake warned. Tens of thousands of these laborers died in the Battle of the Somme (60,000 the first day) because, among other rea-
sons, their officers thought them too stupid to attack in any way
other than marching straight up, row on row, into the German
guns. Contemporary memoirist Edmund Blunden wrote of "the
battle that neither race had won, nor could win, the War. The War
had won, and would go on winning." One of the Somme casualities
was meliorism, and the Victorian perception of history as "a coherent stream of time running from past through present to future" (Fussell's phrase) was fragmented forever. See
MODERNISM.

**metaphor**   Whereas a simile is a comparison, using "like" or "as," of two ostensibly dissimilar objects, a metaphor is a direct equation of the two. Consider the difference in force between the statements "you are like a pig" or "you are as fat as a pig" (similes) and "you are a fat pig" (metaphor). A characteristic of the metaphor is its concision; as one character tells another in Robertson Davies's novel *The Manticore*, "I use metaphor to spare you jargon."

**metaphysics**   The study of the ultimate nature of existence. Metaphysics includes the basic concerns of ONTOLOGY but may entertain theological and cosmological questions as well.

**method, the**   A system of dramatic training that eliminates artificial and mechanical techniques and emphasizes performance based on an actor's own experience; developed in Russia by Constantin Stanislavsky and promoted in America by Lee Strasberg, whose students included James Dean, Marlon Brando, and Marilyn Monroe. W. T. Lhamon notes that "this new trolling in the gut for deep form influenced and coincided with movements in the other arts," including jazz, beat poetry, and ABSTRACT EXPRESSIONISM.

**mind-body problem**   A concern with the existence or absence of a dichotomy between mind and body. There are four principal possibilities for a mind-body relationship: (1) all is mind, (2) all is body, (3) mind and body exist separately but interact, and (4) mind and body exist separately and function separately.

**minimalism**   An art term of the 1960s that describes work in which expression is minimized almost to the point of being eliminated entirely; an outgrowth of FORMALISM. Because minimalism begs to be justified, it generates a critical response disproportionate to the size of the work itself. The art critic Harold Rosenberg (quoted in Calvin Tomkins's *Off the Wall*) com-

plains that " 'the rule applied is: The less there is to see, the more
there is to say.' Three boards nailed together and hung on a wall
'could yield an almost inexhaustible supply of the aesthetic minuti-
ae discovered in Minimal masterworks.' " See CONCEPTUAL-
ISM.


**Möbius strip**   Taking its name from eighteenth-century
German mathematician and astronomer August Ferdinand
Möbius, the Möbius band or strip is a solid body that has only one
side, though it seems to have two. A Möbius strip is easily made
by cutting a long, thin strip of paper, giving it a single twist, and
gluing the ends together. A line drawn down the middle of the
strip eventually meets itself; there is no need to turn the strip
over, and, indeed, it cannot be done. Similarly, the strip cannot be
cut in two—whether the cut is made across the band or around it,
one ends up with a single body. Möbius strips are of interest to
students of topology (the study of bodies that remain invariant under certain transformations) and also to practically anyone in any
field who puzzles over beginnings and endings. The Dutch artist
Maurits Escher frequently incorporated Möbius strips into his
ironic, implausible drawings. And contemporary author Gabriel
Josipovici's "Möbius the Stripper: A Topological Exercise" appears in two parts that are separated horizontally: the top half is
the story proper, and the bottom half is the narrator's account of
his struggle to write the story. Does one read both parts concur-
rently, or the first from start to finish, then the second? It would
be logical to read the second part and then the first, the "history"
of the story and then the story itself, yet the work appears on the
page in a way that does not invite such an approach. Where does
"Möbius the Stripper" begin, and where does it end?


**modernism**   A movement in the arts characterized generally by technical experimentation and the rejection of traditional
forms. Paul Fussell dates the start of the modernist period from
the passing of the Military Service Act in 1916, when England began to train her first conscript army; by common consent, modernism came to an end with the detonation of the first atomic bomb

over Hiroshima in 1945. In the meantime, says Peter Gay, there occurred "a pervasive cultural revolution, a second Renaissance. . . . Modernism transformed culture in all its branches. It utterly changed painting, sculpture, and music; the dance, the novel, and the drama; architecture, poetry, and thought. And its ventures into unknown territory percolated from the rarefied regions of high culture to general ways of thinking, feeling, and seeing. A very troop of masters compelled Western civilization to alter its angle of vision, and to adopt a new aesthetic sensibility, a new philosophical style, a new mode of understanding social life and human nature."

In the classical view, art had a unifying social function, and the artist was regarded as one who arranged words or paint in a way that both expressed and affected the culture. But modernism's emphasis on aesthetics and on the alienated condition of the artist changed all that. George P. Elliott points out that "instead of seeing art as a form of magic and an artist as a wizard arranging physical things so as to affect the souls of others, aesthetics said that a true 'object' of art was so pure it had neither moral power nor social function—in effect, was not a necessity but an adornment to life. . . . By denying any life-or-death potency to art, the Modern Age made all true artists, even the few it appreciated, feel rejected or neglected, cut off from the body politic. However, because the age prided itself on its liberality, it left artists free to counterattack. Many of the great ones set their lives and best work against their age (as artists in previous epochs have almost never done) and also elevated The Artist as superior to other types of men."

The difference between CLASSICISM and modernism is the difference between transition and juxtaposition, according to Roger Shattuck. The use of the conjunction in grammar and rhetoric, of perspective in painting, of harmonic progression in music—these connected one moment to the next. In the arts of the twentieth century, one thing is simply set down next to another without connective. A forceful style of juxtaposition first broke out "like a rash" in the writings of such French authors as "Apollinaire, Cendrars, and Reverdy. They recorded the world in the still-scrambled order of sensation," says Shattuck, "and the style soon affected the work of Ezra Pound, Wyndham Lewis, Virginia Woolf, James Joyce, and Valéry Larbaud." The preeminent work of modern literature, of course, is Eliot's *The Waste Land* (1922). *The Waste Land* is notoriously recondite, but John Barth says that "if modernist works are often forbidding and require a fair amount of help and training to appreciate, it does not follow that they are not superbly rewarding, as climbing Mount Matterhorn must be, or sailing a small boat around the world." See ANTIMODERNISM, MELIORISM, and POSTMODERNISM.

**monism**  Any philosophical system that views all phenomena as a unified whole; the opposite of DUALISM. Typically detached, passive, and contemplative, the serious monist is likely to practice a form of QUIETISM as well.

**montage**  In film, a technique in which two or more shots are combined for a single effect, as when a man jumps off what appears to be a high building (actually a low parapet built a few feet off the ground) and strikes the sidewalk a few seconds later.

André Bazin gives an example of an effective bit of camera work using montage. In an "otherwise mediocre" English film entitled *Where No Vultures Fly*, Bazin isolates one memorable sequence. The film concerns a young couple who manage a game reserve in South Africa and who live in the wilds with their small child. The notable sequence is something of a cinematic cliché: the child, wandering alone in the jungle, discovers a temporarily abandoned lion cub and decides to take it for a pet. The lioness, discovering the absence of the cub, sets out after the imprudent lad. The pursuit is shown in parallel montage: first a shot of the boy with the cub, then a shot of the lioness, and so on until pursuer and pursued reach the campground. To this point, according to Bazin, the sequence is a conventional and "somewhat naïve attempt at suspense. . . . Then suddenly, to our horror, the director abandons his montage of separate shots that has kept the protagonists apart and gives us instead parents, child, and lioness all in the same shot." Trickery is abandoned. The viewer sees the father ordering the boy to put the cub on the ground, the lioness picking up the cub and moving off quietly into the bush—all in the same shot. In this case montage is used so that it can be deliberately subverted for effect.

**Morellian method**   A method of authenticating paintings.
Nineteenth-century art critic Giovanni Morelli based his theory of
authentication on an examination of such details as earlobes and
fingernails. His reasoning was that whereas most masters relied
on formulas for such details, thinking that no connoisseur would
care, few forgers would take the trouble to execute such details
with any precision at all, much less according to formula.

**mysticism**   Personal experience of the divine or of the har-
mony of the universe or of both; a joyful state beyond reason, beyond ordinary sensory experience, beyond time. The great complaint about the mystical state is that it cannot be described, but
the same is true of the most mundane experiences as well, e.g.,
the taste of steak.

**myth**   An anonymously authored story of supernatural occurrences that accounts for some aspect of a people's world view. In
*The Masks of God*, Joseph Campbell discusses five myths that
have persisted throughout history, the stories of the theft of fire,
the cataclysmic event (such as the Biblical flood), the land of the
dead, the virgin birth, and the resurrected hero. See ARCHE-
TYPE, COLLECTIVE UNCONSCIOUS.

# N

**natural law**  The body of laws that naturally underlie every culture, as opposed to, say, the revealed law of a given religion or the law of authority imposed by a tyrant. Fairness, justice, and the advancement of the common good are all tenets of natural law, regardless of the varied forms they take in different legal systems.

**natural selection**  The biological process whereby only organisms that are able to adapt to an environment survive; the principle underlying EVOLUTION. See also NEO-DARWINISM and QUANTUM SPECIATION.

**naturalism**  An intensification of REALISM in which realistic technique is used to describe life from the Darwinian standpoint of NATURAL SELECTION. Whereas the realist can report objectively and dispassionately on almost any subject, the naturalist prefers to see life as a struggle, usually between some ill-equipped protagonist and an all-powerful antagonist: God, nature, fate, heredity, environment, another human or group of humans. A common image in naturalistic fiction is the machine, which may represent an economic system as in Frank Norris's "A Deal of Wheat" (1903), a battle as in Stephen Crane's *The Red Badge of Courage* (1895), or any other entity that is self-sufficient, indifferent, and unresponsive to the protagonists—except to destroy them should they come too near.

Since the protagonist is to be crushed more often than not, it is to the naturalist's advantage to focus on the weak person, the loser, the drunkard, the dolt. In an 1894 sketch by Stephen Crane entitled "Mr. Binks' Day Off: A Study of a Clerk's Holiday," the protagonist takes his family to the country for the weekend. Swinging his arm wide at the wondrousness of nature, Bunks says, "I wonder why . . . I wonder why the dickens it—why it—why—." There is more to be said, but Binks cannot say it. Life is too big for him.

In addition to its implicit support of Darwin's theory of man's relative insignificance in the chain of life, naturalism has a considerable scientific and philosophic pedigree, especially on the European continent. In 1830 Auguste Comte began publishing his *Cours de Philosophie Positive*, in which he argued that through the ages knowledge had developed from the theological to the metaphysical to the scientific, from the fictitious to the abstract to the positive. In 1865 Claude Bernard extended Comte's POSITIVISM in his *Introduction a l'Etude de la Médecine Experimentale*, arguing that human functions can be explained solely by the interactions of the various chemical elements in the body. It was this view that Emile Zola adopted in *Le Roman Experimental* (1880), where he offered the novel as a literary "experiment" equal to any scientific one.

Unfortunately, the self-proclaimed scientism of the naturalists is skewed by their foreknowledge of the outcome of their "experiments" and their need to focus on the downtrodden in order to demonstrate the fatalistic nature of life. Thus there are relatively few pure works of naturalism. On the other hand, the naturalistic themes of struggle and defeat are pervasive in modern literature; Edmund Wilson has pointed out that the history of twentieth-century literature is largely the history of the interplay between SYMBOLISM and naturalism. See DETERMINISM.


**negative capability**    In a letter of December 21, 1817, to his brothers George and Thomas, John Keats wrote of the quality that formed any "Man of Achievement . . . I mean *Negative Capability*, that is when a man is capable of being in uncertainties, mysteries, doubts, without any irritable reaching after fact and reason." Negative capability suggests both patience and flexibility, and implicitly the phrase warns against the mistakes that result, as Keats says later in the same letter, "from being incapable of remaining content with half-knowledge."

**neoclassicism**  A resurgence of the principles of CLASSICISM in the eighteenth century. The period variously called the Age of Reason, the Augustan Age, the Enlightenment, the Classical Period (in France), or the Neoclassical (in England) was an age in which literature, philosophy, political theory, and science put humankind at the center of a universe that had been set in motion long since by a remote God, a God who had then left the universe—and humankind itself—the prime and perhaps the only subject worthy of scrutiny. This anthropocentric view leads inevitably to a certain self-congratulation in thought and letters, to an elegance in expression as well as a bluffness in point of view that reaches its height in the writings of authors as different as Samuel Johnson and Voltaire.

**Neo-Darwinism**  Essentially Darwin's idea of NATURAL SELECTION updated to include the ideas of genetics. According to the Neo-Darwinists, natural selection and genetics together explain the development of the various life forms into their present states.

**Neoplatonism**  Any modification of PLATONISM, especially Plotinus' belief in a single, all-sufficient unity from which all lesser entities emanate. Historically, Neoplatonism is the bridge between Plato's thought and mainstream Christianity.

**neurosis**  A class of mental and emotional disturbances that includes anxiety, depression, obsession, hysteria, etc.; less severe than PSYCHOSIS.

**New Criticism**  Facetiously yet accurately called the "lemon-squeezing school" of literary criticism, the New Criticism examines the text as an object in itself, excluding the author's life and times and all other extratextual considerations; it looks instead at the work's images, symbols, and word usages in the context of the work itself, and only in that context.

In large part, the New Criticism supersedes the purely scholarly approach to literature. To give an example: a literary scholar encountering the last lines of Robert Browning's "My Last Duchess" (". . . Notice Neptune, though, / Taming a seahorse, thought a rarity, / Which Claus of Innsbruck cast in bronze for me!") would gloss Neptune, observe that Claus is either a fictional or an unidentifiable sculptor, and let it go at that. A New Critic, on the other hand, would elaborate the symbolic value of the reference, pointing out that the Duke is presenting one more image of genteel brutality, one more reminder of the chilling yet paradoxically attractive and artfully constructed mask that he has shown the reader throughout the poem.

The sources of the New Criticism include I. A. Richards's *The Principles of Literary Criticism* (1924), William Empson's *Seven Types of Ambiguity* (1930), the essays of T.S. Eliot, and the French tradition of the *explication de texte*. The New Criticism is still important today as a complement to HISTORICAL CRITICISM and as an antidote to purely impressionistic reactions to literature. Too, it established critical writing as a genre in itself, making possible a variety of interpretative schools that have succeeded the New Criticism and sometimes denigrate it. See AFFECTIVE FALLACY, AMBIGUITY, and INTENTIONAL FALLACY.


**New History**   Whereas traditional history is narrative and concerns itself with major figures and events, the so-called New History of the 1960s and thereafter is primarily analytic and quantitative and concerned with groups. As C. Vann Woodward says, the New Historians "turned from the public to the private sector: to the family, the nursery, the bedroom, the deathbed and their psychological secrets; to demography and long-term shifts in population, marriage, birth rates and sex roles; to popular culture; to the history of prisons, hospitals, villages, cities and churches; to voting behavior as prompted by ethnic and religious rather than public, issues." The traditional and the new approaches are hardly mutually exclusive, of course. For example, new historical methods might be applied to learn more about the popular support (or lack of it) for a political leader.

A typical work of the New History school is Richard Cobb's *Death in Paris*, which is based on civil records describing 404 violent deaths between October 1795 and mid-September 1801. Cobb's analysis, particularly of the depositions taken from those who knew the deceased (at least four respondents per corpse), reveal a picture far less gloomy than the title of his study suggests. As Cobb concludes, "Even the most deprived—especially the most deprived—set store by certain acceptable rules of conduct that enriched a brutal and often monotonous life with the reassurance of habit and the priceless gifts of companionship and conversation." In this way the New History attempts to illuminate the lives of the masses, how they suffered and how they transcended their suffering.

**New Humanism**   A conservative and ethical movement in American philosophy and literary criticism in the 1920s. Led by Irving Babbitt, Paul Elmer More, and Norman Foerster, the New Humanism was a reaction agaihst NATURALISM and it stressed the moral qualities of literature. Eventually it gave way to Marxist and Freudian approaches to literature and to the NEW CRITICISM.

**New Novel**   See NOUVEAU ROMAN.

**nihilism**   The rejection of traditional values and established laws. Coined by Ivan Turgenev in his novel *Fathers and Sons* (1862), the term nihilism describes the principles of a Russian revolutionary group that held that extant society must be destroyed before a new and untainted order could be established; hence the frequent equation of nihilism with terrorist activity and vice versa.

Philosophically, nihilism is associated with the philosophy of

Nietzsche, who thought that the future would see the triumph of nihilism. In *Time of Need*, William Barrett asserts that "the history of our century could be written as the encounter of our century with Nihilism, which now assumes guises and disguises that Nietzsche, bound to his own times, could not have foreseen in detail." For instance, there is "the Nihilism of Conformism, which no longer believes wholeheartedly in the routines that sustain it," just as there is the "Nonconformism that may cast itself in the role of idealistic rebellion while in fact it harbors a nihilistic core and is driven secretly by an adolescent lust for destruction." According to Barrett, the philosophy of our time that opposes nihilism is EXISTENTIALISM. See DADA.

**noetic**    From the Greek *noetikos* "intelligent," a philosophical term referring to the function of reason and the intellect; opposed to ANOETIC and similar in meaning to the psychological term CONSCIOUS.

**nominalism**    The belief that abstract concepts have only names, not essences. Nominalism is the opposite of philosophical realism, which argues that abstract concepts do have objective essences. Conceptualism, a compromise between these two beliefs, says that abstract concepts have specific essences that we conceptualize when we create names for them.

**noncommutative mathematics**    See COMMUTATIVE MATHEMATICS.

**nouveau roman**    A type of ANTINOVEL as written by Alain Robbe-Grillet, Nathalie Sarraute, Michel Butor, and others. The *nouveau roman* opposes the linear narrative of the traditional novel with a chaotic and nonsequential reportage; instead of a metaphorical style, it offers a flat, journalistic one.

In its subversion of classic novel form, this "new novel" has won as many enemies as friends. The *nouveau roman* has been described with grudging whimsicality by John Perreault as always "cold, boring, intellectual, plotless, and in French." And George P. Elliott complains that whereas when he reads traditional fiction he gets a strong, clear sense of the author, after reading Robbe-Grillet's *The Voyeur* (1955) he comes away with only "a blurred, hollow sense of the person who made it." No doubt that is M. Robbe-Grillet's intent. See POSTMODERNISM.

**nova**   See STELLAR EVOLUTION.

**numinous**   The aspect of religious or supernatural experience that engenders awe in the beholder. The numinous, which may be described by the Latin phrase *mysterium tremendum et fascinans* (a frightening but entrancing mystery), does not provoke fear, exactly, but something like it, though harder to define. C. S. Lewis describes the sensation this way: "Suppose you were told there was a tiger in the next room; you would know that you were in danger and would probably feel fear. But if you were told 'There is a ghost in the next room,' and believed it, you would feel, indeed, what is often called fear, but of a different kind. It would be based on the knowledge of danger, for no one is primarily afraid of what a ghost may do to him, but of the mere fact that it is a ghost."

# O

**objective correlative**   An object, situation, or event in a work of art that evokes the desired response in the beholder. In his 1919 essay "Hamlet and His Problems," T.S. Eliot complained that the play was a failure because there was no objective correlative in it sufficient to justify Hamlet's attitudes and behavior.

**objectivism**   Philosophical belief that reality exists externally and independent of our perception of it; the opposite of SOLIPSISM.

**Occam's razor**   A tool for shaving away inapplicable explanations, Occam's razor advises the logician to select the simplest cause for any phenomenon, the cause that needs the least justification. Formulated by a fourteenth-century Franciscan scholar named William of Occam, the principle reads thus in Latin: *Entia non sunt multiplicanda praeter necessitatem*, or "Entities are not to be multiplied unnecessarily." As medical diagnosticians say, when you hear hooves, look for horses, not zebras.

   Occam is sometimes spelled Ockham or Ockam, and Occam's razor is sometimes called the principle of parsimony or the principle of simplicity or the principle of economy.

**ontology**   The study of what exists (as opposed to what appears to exist but does not). MATERIALISM and IDEALISM are two opposed ontological theories. See METAPHYSICS.

**organicism**   See HOLISM.

**oscillating infinite series**   See INFINITE SERIES.

**oxymoron**   A figure of speech in which contradictory terms are combined, as in "thunderous silence."

# P

**Papez-MacLean theory**   A physiologically based theory
of our confused emotional makeup. The brain is like an orange: the
central part is the pulp or medulla, which is a prolongation of the
spinal cord, and the outer portion is the rind or cortex. The cortex
itself has three subdivisions with overlapping functions:
physiologist Paul MacLean calls them the archicortex or reptilian
brain; the mesocortex or paleo-mammalian (early mammalian)
brain; and the neocortex or neo-mammalian (later mammalian)
brain. While other body parts evolved cleanly—flippers became
arms, for example, and gills turned into lungs—the cortex was
simply added onto. The reptilian brain rather coldly tends to such
simple matters as survival and the obtaining of food, the paleo-
mammalian brain is passionate and capable of both anger and sexual love, and the neo-mammalian brain is responsible for such
higher functions as contemplation and insight. Poet Robert Bly
says, "As the reptile brain power is symbolized by cold, and the
mammal brain by warmth, the mark of the new brain is light." According to MacLean, we may speak allegorically of these three
brains within a brain by imagining "that when the psychiatrist
bids the patient to lie on the couch, he is asking him to stretch out
alongside a horse and a crocodile." The patient who is trying sin-
cerely to articulate his or her deepest emotions must simultaneously speak for the crocodile, the horse, and the higher primate.
Hence the Papez-MacLean theory: while the arm knows that it is
only an arm and the lungs never try to behave like gills, the "brain"
is actually three brains at once, and, with no clear, hierarchic governance, it produces emotional confusion and conflict. MacLean

notes it is "little wonder that the patient who has personal responsibility for these animals and who must serve as their mouthpiece is sometimes accused of being full of resistances and reluctant to talk."

People with poor control over their three brains are liable to suffer from such emotional problems as PARANOIA, which is the result of unregulated activity in the archicortex (in the absence of enemies, the reptile brain will invent imaginary ones so that it will have something to conquer). On the other hand, improved control over the three brains is the key to great art; in *The Ghost in the Machine*, Arthur Koestler notes that "poetry could . . . be said to achieve a synthesis between the sophisticated reasoning of the neocortex and the more primitive emotional ways of the old brain." To Bly, it is a matter of encouraging the transfer of energy from the reptile brain to the mammalian to the new brain. "If the body sits in a room for an hour, quietly, doing nothing, the reptile brain becomes increasingly restless. It wants excitement, danger. . . . Of course if the sitter continues to sit, the mammal brain quickly becomes restless too. It wants excitement, confrontations, insults, sexual joy. It now starts to feed in spectacular erotic imagery, of the sort that St. Anthony's sittings were famous for. Yet if the sitter persists in doing nothing, eventually energy has nowhere to go but to the new brain." Since we do not spend all day in a single brain but flip back and forth constantly from one to another, the secret is to be aware of the flips, to bring the deep ancestral images of the reptile brain and the fiery passions of the mammal brain up into the well-lit chambers of the new brain, where they can be examined, sequenced, and revised. Koestler uses a French phrase to describe this artistic process, *reculer pour mieux sauter*—falling back in order to leap forward.


**paradigm**   A model; specifically, a coherent tradition of scientific research, such as Copernican astronomy or Newtonian physics. The establishment of a paradigm marks the achievement of maturity by a particular branch of science, yet it does not mean stasis. Thomas S. Kuhn points out that whereas a grammatical paradigm is the basis for replication (knowing how to conjugate one regular verb in Latin means knowing how to conjugate a large number of similar verbs), a scientific paradigm, "like an accepted judicial decision in the common law, . . . is an object for further articulation and specification under new or more stringent conditions."

It is the paradoxical nature of paradigms, this mature yet constantly tested state, that leads to progress. According to Ernest Gellner, Kuhn claimed that "obedience to a paradigm . . . was the precondition of a scientific community and its cumulative work" because "if each worker on the great scientific enterprise feels ever free and inclined to re-open . . . issues, nothing much gets done, even if it fails to be done at the highest and deepest intellectual level." For the same reason, when a paradigm dies, it dies in several places at once. As Kuhn notes, "The very fact that a significant scientific novelty so often emerges simultaneously from several laboratories is an index both to the strongly traditional nature of normal science and to the completeness with which that traditional pursuit prepares the way for its own change." See GEDANKEN EXPERIMENT.


**paranoia**   A form of PSYCHOSIS characterized by delusions of either persecution or grandeur or both ("they're out to get me because I am a superior being"). When the delusions become persistent and take the form of hallucinations, the condition becomes paranoid schizophrenia.

Though it generally has a negative connotation, paranoia can also be positive in nature. In *The Natural Mind*, Andrew Weil notes that paranoia consists of the imposition of a pattern on random events and then—usually—the hostile interpretation of that pattern. But Weil cites a number of paranoid test subjects who, while typically finding meaning in every blot of a RORSCHACH TEST, saw their findings as proof "that the universe is a conspiracy organized for their own benefit." (In sports, says Geoffrey Stokes, this tendency is commonly called "a winning attitude.") See SCHIZOPHRENIA and, for some of the causes that may underlie paranoia, see PAPEZ-MACLEAN THEORY and REACTION-FORMATION.


**paranoid schizophrenia**   See both PARANOIA and SCHIZOPHRENIA.

**parody**   A caricature or burlesque of some serious subject. Whereas the intent of SATIRE is to expose and discredit, the intent of parody is to ridicule; in his book, *S.J. Perelman*, Douglas Fowler notes that "satire is a weapon, but parody is a toy."

**Pascal's Wager**   According to Pascal, you may as well believe in God: by betting on His existence, you have everything to win if He does exist and nothing to lose if He does not. Call it afterlife insurance. Presumably God would know what you are up to, but then there must be places in heaven for the merely shrewd.

**passive-aggressive behavior**   Seemingly passive behavior (e.g., stubbornness,indecision, pouting) directed by an individual toward someone on whom he or she is overly dependent.

**pathetic fallacy**   The attribution of emotions to natural phenomena. In *Modern Painters* (1843), John Ruskin quotes these lines from Charles Kingsley's "Alton Lock": "They rowed her in across the rolling foam— / The cruel, crawling foam," then notes acerbically that "the foam is not cruel, neither does it crawl." The problem, says Ruskin, is that "violent feelings . . . produce in us a falseness in all our impulses of external things, which I would generally characterize as the 'pathetic fallacy.' " A weeping willow only appears to be sad.

**persistence of vision**   The retention on the retina of an image. Conventionally film moves at a speed of twenty-four frames per second, and while the eye cannot isolate any single frame, each frame presents an image that does not fade completely before the next frame is seen, thus providing the effect of continuity where none actually exists. A physiological occurrence, persistence of vision results in a psychological perception of movement called the phi phenomenon by GESTALT psychologists.

**persona**   Literally the Latin word for "mask," a persona is the unidentified first-person speaker in poetry. When Yeats says,

"I will arise and go now, and go to Innisfree, / And a small cabin build there," it is a persona speaking and not Yeats, who stayed home and wrote poetry. A convenient means for setting aside the poet's private personality and its potential for confusing the reader's understanding of a work, the persona concept may be applied to fiction as well as to the lives of public figures, both literary and nonliterary. People as different as Walt Whitman and Winston Churchill clearly constructed the personae that others expected them to wear.

**personification**   The representation as human of something that is not. For example, in his ode "To Autumn," Keats depicts the season as a farmer harvesting his crop and watching the juice ooze from a cider press.

**perspective**   The method whereby three-dimensional objects are represented credibly on the flat surface of a painting or drawing. See FORESHORTENING.

**phenomenology**   A method of inquiry propounded by philosopher Edmund Husserl in which pure phenomena are examined and described and everything else—possible causes, effects, wider implications—are "bracketed" or eliminated from consideration. In *Time of Need*, William Barrett quotes Husserl's slogan *"Zu den Sachen selbst!"* ("To the things themselves!") as well as the words of Husserl's follower Martin Heidegger, who said, "Thinking must learn again to descend into the poverty of its materials."

Husserl insisted that his method was not empirical and that he was attempting an intuitive seizure of essences common to all phenomena of a certain class. By thus emphasizing the search for the authentic heart of any experience, phenomenology reveals not only its roots in APRIORISM but also its effect on the development of EXISTENTIALISM and STRUCTURALISM.

**phi phenomenon**   See PERSISTENCE OF VISION.

**Platonism, platonic** The philosophy of Plato, especially the idea that the true forms of things are heavenly in nature and that the earthly forms are but debased versions of these ideals. Thus the adjective platonic means "ideal," in the sense that a platonic meal, for example, is perfect, the kind a god would eat. In the phrase "platonic love," however, the adjective has a more specialized meaning and signifies a spiritual relationship, one that is devoid of the messiness of sexual urgency. See NEOPLATONISM.

**pleasure principle** The instinct to seek pleasure and avoid pain. Freud recalls that when he wet his bed as a child it was his father who reproved him, not his mother. Thus Ernest Jones, Freud's colleague and biographer, says that "it was from such experiences that was born Freud's conviction that typically it was the father who represented to his son the principles of denial, restraint, restriction, and authority; the father stood for the reality principle, the mother for the pleasure principle."

But Freud himself noted in *Beyond the Pleasure Principle*: "From the point of view of the self-preservation of the organism among the difficulties of the external world, the pleasure principle is from the very outset inefficient and even highly dangerous. Under the influence of the ego's instincts of self-preservation, the pleasure principle is replaced by the *reality principle*." See CONSTANCY PRINCIPLE, EGO, ID, and REALITY PRINCIPLE.

**poesia ermetica** See HERMETIC.

**pointillism** A neoimpressionist development, pointillism reflects the scientific interests of Georges Seurat, whose paintings consist of tiny "points" of unmixed primary colors, the idea being that the viewer's eye will combine the little dots to form images. Seurat not only studied optics and spectroscopy but endeavored to emulate the scientist in such matters as his rigid work schedule and his attempts to develop his technique programmatically. See IMPRESSIONISM.

**Poisson distribution**   Named for the nineteenth-century French mathematician Siméon Denis Poisson, this distribution applies to events that are highly improbable when a great number of trials occur, such as traffic deaths at a given intersection where there are thousands of "trials" every day yet very few accidents severe enough to cause death.

The Poisson distribution illustrates well the possibility for uncanny stability in PROBABILITY THEORY. Warren Weaver gives the following example: "The circumstances which result in a dog biting a person seriously enough so that the matter gets reported to the health authorities would seem to be complex and unpredictable indeed. But in New York City, in the year 1955, there were, on the average, 75.3 reports per day to the Department of Health of bitings of people. In 1956 the corresponding number was 73.6 In 1957 it was 73.2. In 1957 and 1958 the figures were 74.5 and 72.6." See also GAUSSIAN DISTRIBUTION.

**polymorphous perversity**   The child's indiscriminate and anarchistic exploration of the body's erotic potential. If we rid ourselves of the pejorative connotations of the word "perversity," says Norman O. Brown, we will accept polymorphous perversity as "the pattern of our deepest desires," desires blunted in adult life by the REALITY PRINCIPLE. This conflict between the desires of infant sexuality (which survive in the fantasies and dreams of grownups) and the demands of adult behavior is the central problem in Freudian psychology.

**positivism**   The belief that knowledge is scientific in nature, i.e., based on the description of observable phenomena only; the scientific form of EMPIRICISM. Positivism was given its name by Auguste Comte, who propounded a system that concerned itself with existing facts and excluded speculation on extraneous matters (see NATURALISM).

Positivists are oblivious to the past, to what they have learned in school and what tradition may tell them. When the mocking hero of e. e. cummings's *The Enormous Room* (1922) sees a roadside crucifix in France, he observes not Christ the Savior but "a little wooden man hanging all by himself" and asks, "Who was this wooden man?" Commenting on this scene in cummings's novel, Paul Fussell says, "This is Positivism with a vengeance."

## *post hoc ergo propter hoc*

*post hoc ergo propter hoc*   Literally the Latin for "after this, therefore the cause of this," *post hoc ergo propter hoc* is a fallacy based on a false notion of causality; it argues that something happened only because something else occurred earlier. Lawyers seem to be especially fond of this form of reasoning; for example, if a defense attorney argues that a client should be forgiven the offense because he or she suffered from abuse during infancy, the prosecutor might offer either a conflicting argument (e.g., that the defendant enjoyed a comfortable and well-adjusted adolescence and therefore had no excuse for the crime) or a deliberately silly one designed to expose the fallacious thinking of the defense attorney (e.g., that the defendant ate a certain breakfast cereal every day for a month before committing a crime that may as well be attributed to this antecedent behavior as any other). Most superstitions involve a form of *post hoc ergo propter hoc* thought, for example, the notion that if one walks under a ladder, then something terrible will happen.

## *postmodernism*

*postmodernism*   An intensification of MODERNISM, the idea being that human perception underwent wrenching changes at the turn of the century and then again in the late 1950s. Modernism begins with disbelief in what Jean-François Lyotard and others call the meta-narrative, the "great narrative" or structure that underlies and validates all other structures. As scientific knowledge came to be seen as another form of discourse by humanists, the concerns of modernism became both broader and deeper, and the whole question of the legitimation of knowledge— the validation of one perception rather than another—became all the more difficult.

In the arts, postmodernism results in an opposition to such underlying principles of order as symbolism, which gives structure even to a work as superficially fragmented as *The Waste Land* (1922). The NOUVEAU ROMAN is a representative postmodern form.

**poststructuralism**   See DECONSTRUCTION.


**pragmatism**   The philosophical belief that the value of an idea is determined only by its effect, that experimental results alone can determine the truth or validity of a proposition, that the meaning of an idea is determined by the uses to which it can be put and the consequences stemming from such use. Pragmatism was developed by three American philosophers (C. S. Peirce, William James, and John Dewey) and is often described as an especially apt philosophy for a country whose national character is so strongly determined by the frontiering process; as Frederick Jackson Turner and subsequent historians have pointed out, the American penchant for practicality—and, concomitantly, American disdain for culture and history—is related directly to the demands of the ever-moving frontier. See EMPIRICISM and POSITIVISM.


**preconscious**   See SUBCONSCIOUS.


**prime number**   See REUCTIO AD ABSURDUM.


**primitivism**   In the visual arts, a deliberate avoidance of sophistication, as in the jungle paintings of Henri Rousseau; generally, a return to the primal.

Of course, there is something paradoxical and perhaps ludicrous about a great mind's descent into the mud. In *Time of Need*, William Barrett draws a distinction between what he calls Alexandrianism and primitivism in the writings of James Joyce. Alexandria became the center of culture in the ancient world when Greek culture slipped into its decline. But the Alexandrians were scholars rather than poets, so they researched Homer, interpreted him, footnoted him, and anthologized him along with other authors of Greek history and myth. "But the more they labored at these scholarly tasks," says Barrett, "the further the myth receded from them." This tension between the primitive and the pedantic informs Joyce's entire career and reaches its peak in his last great work. Barrett says that "the paradox of *Finnegans Wake* is that while it aims to tell the story of Everyman and thus appeal to the most elemental emotions, it is written in a language that draws out the hidden pedant in all of us."

According to Stanley Kunitz, the poet Lionel Johnson told Yeats, "You need ten years in the library, but I have need of ten years in a wilderness." Says Kunitz: "The library and the wilderness, order and disorder, reason and madness, technique and imagination—the poet to be complete must polarize the contradictions."

**probability theory**   The theory that seeks to predict the general outcome of processes (sometimes called stochastic processes) consisting of large numbers of particular outcomes, each of which in itself cannot be predicted. A simple example involves a coin toss. The chances of the coin coming up heads are fifty-fifty; even if it comes up heads ninety-nine times in a row, the odds of the coin coming up heads on the hundredth toss are still fifty-fifty, because each toss is a discrete act, not causally related to the ones preceding it. But the more the coin is tossed, the greater the probability of it showing heads about half the time and tails the rest.

Hence the need for a great number of individual instances in any kind of probability test. In *The Roots of Coincidence*, Arthur Koestler gives the example of an extrasensory-perception text in which the so-called law of great numbers is manifest. A subject is guessing at a hundred consecutive cards that are being turned up one by one by an experimenter in another room; there are five types of cards, so he should make twenty correct guesses in his hundred tries. When the subject makes twenty-two guesses, no one is impressed, because the odds against such a result are not significantly challenged. But suppose the subject goes on, consistently scoring 10 percent better than the odds predict, as he has done above. By 1,000 guesses, he has made 220 correct guesses instead of 200; the odds against this result are six to one. By 5,000 guesses, he has still done 10 percent better than expected and has scored 1,100 times instead of 1,000; the odds are 2,000 to one against such an outcome. After 10,000 guesses, the subject has been right a consistent 2,200 times instead of a mere 2,000. Since the odds against this being attributable to chance are now 2 million to one, the experimenters may conclude that their subject does indeed have unusual gifts.

Probability theory has its origin in the speculations of one Antoine Gombauld, Chevalier de Méré, Sieur de Baussay, a seventeenth-century philosopher and gambler who was fond of a certain game of dice. The Chevalier took his not not-wholly-disinterested concerns to the young Blaise Pascal, a friend of his, who subsequently developed the basis for the mathematical theory of probability in an exchange of letters with Pierre de Fermat and in conversations with the Dutch genius Christian Huygens, recently arrived in Paris. Thus, says Warren Weaver, "in the highly fashionable but slightly disreputable atmosphere of the gambling rooms, and announced in the correspondence of French gentlemen of the seventeenth century, Lady Luck was born."

The contemporary application of probability theory to stochastic processes covers everything from the field of education (how many students understand how much of the lesson?) to direct-mail solicitation, in which a 3-percent response to a given mailing is considered highly successful. Probability theory affects the archaeologist looking for a lost city, the geneticist trying to improve the odds on the transmission of certain desirable characteristics, the oil company hoping for a lucky strike. The probabilistic basis of the QUANTUM THEORY and, by extension, of all modern science is well known, and sometimes it is even resented. Einstein's famous statement, "God does not play dice," is the best-known formulation of this minority viewpoint. According to Weaver, "The large majority of scientists, including many truly great ones such as Bohr and Heisenberg, accept the modern reign of probability."


**projection**    The attribution to other persons or to objects of unacceptable traits of one's own. PROJECTIVE TESTS are designed to encourage this tendency for diagnostic purposes.


**projective tests**    See PROJECTION; examples include the

RORSHACH TEST, the THEMATIC APPERCEPTION TEST (TAT), and the WORD-ASSOCIATION TEST.


**prolegomenon**   A prefatory or introductory statement; prolegomena are several such statements. From Greek "to say before."


**propadeutic**   An introductory or preliminary course of instruction, formal or informal; from Greek "to educate before."


**prospect-refuge theory**   The word *prospect* refers to an unlimited opportunity to see, while *refuge* denotes a hiding place. Thus prospect-refuge theory is concerned with the satisfactions that arise from the fulfillment of these two basic needs. *Prospect* and *refuge* appear to be opposites, but they merge in a fundamental biological drive that takes on increasingly sophisticated aspects as one moves into the ranks of the higher primates. Geographer Jay Appleton says that habitat theory deals with our search for an environment capable of satisfying our biological needs, which range all the way from such basic requirements as ingestion and elimination, shelter, and sex to such complex ones as care giving and care seeking. Within such a general theory, "prospect-refuge theory postulates that, because the ability to see without being seen is an intermediate step in the satisfaction of many of these needs, the capacity of an environment to ensure the achievement of *this* becomes a more immediate source of aesthetic satisfaction." To illustrate this fundamental desire to see without being seen and to show that it is a desire that integrates two drives that only appear to be opposed, Appleton quotes Konrad Lorenz's account of shrew behavior. The shrews under observation carefully explore their habitat but spontaneously interrupt their painstaking task of discovery every few moments in order to dash wildly back to the safety of the nest. The shrews are simply assuring themselves that they had not lost their way to a place of refuge and that they could find it again in a matter of seconds if danger arose; according to Lorenz, "It was a queer spectacle to see those

podgy black figures slowly and carefully whisker their way forward and in the next second, with lightning speed, dash back to
the nest-box."

It takes little imagination to see how prospect-refuge theory
might be applied to all sorts of endeavors, from the lonely hobbit's
wistful recollections of his cozy hidey-hole in *The Lord of the
Rings* to the dynamics of interplanetary space travel, with its
seemingly limitless prospect. Appleton's ideas have particular
meaning for the visual arts, and one recalls that the first significant use of landscape in Western art was in Renaissance painting
at a time when the ego found its rightful place in the cosmos and
the great explorers, the prototypes of the brave hobbit and the in-
trepid spaceman, stepped *into* the world and began to look
around. But prospect-refuge theory can also be extended to such
"contrived landscapes" as one's own garden, which is intended to
supply as basic a requirement as food yet which may feature
hedges, grottoes, lovers' nooks, perhaps even a tower from which
"to see without being seen."

**psychosis**    A class of severe mental and emotional illnesses.
While NEUROSIS often refers to a mere exaggeration of some
everyday concern, the psychotic state may be characterized by
such developments as marked personality change, the inability to
distinguish between reality and hallucination, lack of or inappro-
priate emotional response, and so on.

**punctuational model of evolution**    See QUANTUM
SPECIATION.

# Q

**quantum mechanics** The quantum theory and the theory of relativity are the theoretical foundation of modern physics. The quantum theory says that nature is made of bits and pieces; coming as it did in 1900, this new theory made a seam in history, not only between the old and the new science but also between one's sense of the world as an ordered, coherent place and the perception that life is fragmented and disorderly in all its aspects.

Initially the idea of quanta was simply the hypothesis of Max Planck (see BLACK-BODY RADIATION); Michael H. Hart points out that had a less well known and conservative scientist posited the theory it would have been dismissed as a crackpot notion, though by the time Planck received the Nobel Prize in 1918 his theory had been confirmed as fact. Extended and modified by Einstein, Niels Bohr, and others, quantum theory became the basis for quantum mechanics in the 1920s. A "quantum" is a unit of something; "mechanics" refers to the study of energy and forces and their effects on physical bodies. Thus quantum mechanics applies quantum theory to the behavior of particles. Before quantum mechanics, light was thought to be a wave; with its advent, light was seen to be sometimes wavelike and sometimes formed of quanta, discrete little bundles or packets of energy. In this example, quantum theory does not replace the earlier view but simply supplements it: light is seen to retain its wavelike properties while it acquires the new characteristic of discontinuity. The same is true on a larger scale in that classical or Newtonian or macroscopic physics continues to describe accurately the visible universe, while quantum mechanics describes the microscopic world that Newton could not have known. If we were to allow a gram of radium to sit for 1,600 years, for example, we would find the radium diminished by half; that is, there would be half a gram of radium and close to half a gram of lead remaining (some mass loss would occur with the discharge of decay particles). This is predictable and in keeping with Newtonian physics. But it is impossible to know which of the radium atoms are going to disintegrate and which are not; there is no physical law governing this selection, even though there is a physical law that predicts with certainty the disintegration of precisely half the atoms. In this way, the different outlooks of Newtonian physics and quantum mechanics provide us with a complete picture of the world.

According to the 1927 Copenhagen Interpretation of Quantum Mechanics, so called because of the influence of Bohr (from Copenhagen) and his disciples, it is unnecessary to know how things occur, only that they do. As Gary Zukav says, "It is not necessary to know how light can manifest itself both as particles and waves. It is enough to know that it does and to be able to use this phenomenon to predict probabilities. In other words, the wave and particle characteristics of light are unified by quantum mechanics, but at a price. There is no description of reality." Zukav offers a contrast between classical and quantum physics that may be summed up this way: the workings of Newtonian physics may be seen, whereas those of quantum mechanics may not; Newtonian physics is based on ordinary sense perception, whereas quantum mechanics is based on the behavior of subatomic systems that cannot be observed directly; Newtonian physics describes individual things, whereas quantum mechanics describes systems; Newtonian physics predicts events, whereas quantum mechanics predicts possibilities; Newtonian physics assumes an objective reality separate from ourselves, whereas quantum mechanics assumes that our physical reality is our own cognitive construction; Newtonian physics assumes our ability to observe phenomena without changing them, whereas quantum mechanics assumes that any observation will change that which is being observed (see UNCERTAINTY PRINCIPLE). Finally, Newtonian physics claims to be based on absolute truth, while quantum mechanics wants only to correlate experience correctly.

**quantum speciation**   Sometimes called the punctuational model of EVOLUTION, this view opposes the slow and continuous development of species argued by Darwin. Instead, quantum speciation argues that evolution moves in fits and starts, with long periods of little evolution punctuated by periods of brief, rapid change. Darwin faulted the fossil record for not supporting his theory; in *On the Origin of Species by Means of Natural Selection* (1859), he wrote that "the crust of the earth must not be looked at as a well-filled museum, but as a poor collection made at hazard and at rare intervals." At the time, Darwin's dismissal of the fossil record caused the science of paleontology to appear inexact and founded on a shaky empirical basis; now, however, the examination of the same fossil record has provided a case for this new evolutionary model. Paleobiologist Steven Stanley says that "inasmuch as the fossil record is now known well enough to tell us that well-established species undergo little evolution, we are forced to conclude that most evolution has occurred rapidly, within small populations and in local areas—in much the conditions, in fact, under which new types of fruit flies have been developed in the laboratory." (By "rapidly" Stanley means new species may evolve from existing species in less than a thousand years, a mere blink of the eye in geological terms.) Otherwise, says Stanley, what Darwin referred to in *On the Origin of Species* as the "extreme imperfection" of the fossil record is proof that "when, over long stretches of geological time, there is no change in the key aspects of body form that enable us to recognize a species, we can be almost certain that the species underwent no evolution, save for a bit of fine tuning."

**quarks**   Along with leptons, quarks are the most fundamental particles known at present. Quarks form nucleons, which in turn form nuclei and (with electrons) the atoms that combine to make larger structures. The smallest constituent of matter recognized at this time, the quark is so small that none has been observed directly. Its existence was predicted theoretically in 1964 by Murray Gell-Mann, who considered the possibility that nucleons (the smallest known units at that time) consisted of three quarks.

The word itself is taken from *Finnegans Wake* ("three quarks for Muster Mark"). Individual quarks have names like "charm," "strange," "truth," "beauty," and so on; physicist Hans Plendl says that "quarks have ended up with either very silly or very esoteric names—partly because we know so little about them that it does not matter what we name them, partly because we seem to be running out of meaningful names derived from Greek or Latin roots."

Something must be smaller than the quark, of course. As usual, theoretical predictions are well ahead of experimental observations, and speculations abound now in the particle-physics literature on the possible constituents of quarks. As usual, too, the names are ready even though the entity itself has not been observed. The most frequently used name for the particle smaller than the quark is "preon."

**quasar**   See BIG-BANG THEORY.

**quietism**   In its strict religious sense, quietism was founded by a seventeenth-century Spanish priest named Miguel de Molinos, who advocated an effortless and empty state in which the soul would be filled with God's grace and love. In his *Spiritual Guide*, Molinos says that "when God had a mind to instruct His great Captain Moses, and to give him the two Tables of Stone on which the Divine Law was written, He called him up to the Mountain; at what time God being there with him, the Mount was Darkened and environed with thick Clouds, *Moses the while standing quiet without knowledge or power of thought.* . . . So in the Beginning, when God intends after an extraordinary manner, to guide the Soul into the School of Divine and loving Knowledge of the internal Law, He causes her to suffer Darkness, and Dryness, that He may bring her near to Himself, because the Divine Majestie knows very well, that *it is not by the means of her own reasoning or Industry, that a Soul draws near to Him, and understands the Divine Precepts: but rather by silent and humble Resignation*" (emphasis mine).

In a broader sense, quietism is not limited to Christianity or even theism. Quietism may be associated with MONISM in all its variety; whereas monism describes an outlook that occurs in a number of philosophies and religions, quietism describes a kind of behavior, or perhaps it would be better to say nonbehavior.


**QWERTY phenomenon**   The keys of early typewriters were arranged with the ostensible purpose of making them jamproof. Thus letters were put next to other letters that they would not ordinarily precede or follow in normal usage, and, as a result, the top row of lettered keys reads QWERTYUIOP (even though the *-er* combination is a frequent one in English and other languages). This order continues to prevail, even though present-day typewriters have features to keep adjacent keys from jamming. As a result, ARTIFICIAL INTELLIGENCE expert Seymour Papert coined the phrase "QWERTY phenomenon" to refer to any practice that no longer has a rational basis, only a historical one. (In the eighteenth century, Dr. Johnson complained to Boswell that people who followed a belief or superstition that had no current foundation were like the sheep that leap over a nonexistent fence rail because some ancestor of theirs had to leap over a real rail in the past.)

# R

***random walk***   Any process whose future is not dependent on its past; a process without memory. Literally, one takes a random walk by standing on a corner and flipping a coin, turning left on heads and right on tails and repeating the procedure every time one comes to another corner. Since each coin toss is independent of the ones that preceded it (see PROBABILITY THEORY), the process is random.

***reaction-formation***   A tendency that has developed in opposition to a repressed impulse; a common example is seen in the hostility people manifest toward those to whom they are sexually attracted.

Sometimes reaction-formations are quite complex, as in the relationship between PARANOIA and latent homosexuality. Feeling attraction for someone of the same sex, one might experience a reaction-formation: if "I love him" is unacceptable, then "I want to kill him" is better. But "I want to kill him" is still a profoundly disturbing thought, and therefore it may turn into "He wants to kill *me*"—a worrisome notion, yet much less troubling than the two alternatives because it shifts the guilt entirely to the other person.

***reader-response criticism***   In reaction against the AFFECTIVE FALLACY and other tenets of the NEW CRITICISM, reader-response critics are concerned with the relation of text to reader rather than with the text as autonomous object. Steven Mailloux identifies six representative models of reader-response criticism: David Bleich's subjective criticism, Norman Holland's transactive criticism, Wolfgang Iser's phenomenological criticism, Jonathan Culler's structuralist poetics, Stanley Fish's affective stylistics, and Fish's theory of interpretive strategies. According to Mailloux, all of these models share "the phenomenological assumption that it is impossible to separate perceiver from perceived, subject from object. . . . Perception is viewed as interpretive; reading is not the discovery of meaning but the creation of it. Reader-response criticism replaces examinations of a text in-and-of-itself with discussions of the reading process, the 'interaction' of reader and text."

**ready-made**  A mass-produced object made to serve as a work of art, such as the urinal submitted to a New York jury by Marcel Duchamp in 1917. According to DADA theorist Tristan Tzara, art itself was a "parrot word" that could be "replaced by Dada, plesiosaurus, or handkerchief"; therefore why not substitute manufactured objects for created ones? Duchamp maintained that his ready-mades "were mass produced and could be duplicated. . . . In many cases they were duplicated, thus avoiding the cult of uniqueness, of art with a capital 'A.' I consider taste—bad or good—the greatest enemy of art. In the case of the ready-mades, I tried to remain aloof from personal taste and to be fully conscious of the problem. . . . I'm not at all sure that the concept of the ready-made isn't the most important single idea to come out of my work."

Art lovers who find such statements antiartistic will agree with Craig Adcock's observation that "when Duchamp chose a ready-made, he lost his innocence. He was no longer a simple painter, but a philosopher." And those who find Duchamp's shenanigans absurd should remember that, as Adcock says, "such absurdist strategies were born out of despair and were no more absurd than the real events of the world around them. During 1917, a year in which literally hundreds of thousands of young men were dying in the trenches, French soldiers marched in protest through the streets of Paris saying 'Baa, baa' like the sheep led to slaughter that they were." While it is tempting to think of modern art in terms of a long decline from Rembrandt to porcelain urinals, it is more fruitful to see it in terms of the transition from "Baa, baa" to Dada.


**realism**   Although the attempt to portray life realistically reached a peak of sorts in the late nineteenth century, it has always been a significant mode of representation. As Harold H. Kolb Jr. observes, we tend to think of realism as a modern movement, but the *Odyssey* gives descriptions of butchery and boat building that could have been lifted almost verbatim from technical manuals. Too, when we discuss such characters as Chaucer's Wife of Bath or the nurse in *Romeo and Juliet*, we mention invariably the realism with which they are portrayed.

Still, an examination of realism in the arts inevitably leads to a look at the period roughly 1880–1910, when in fact several different "realisms" operated singly or in combination. For example, American literary realism takes at least three distinct forms. Mark Twain practiced a distinctly homely realism marked by frontier humor and LOCAL COLOR in which the bumptious and the uncouth were in full view, and life was shown with all its warts. By contrast, Henry James was a pioneer in psychological realism who diverted the reader's attention from the actions of the plot and focused it instead on his characters' thoughts about those actions. A friend and editor of these two very different authors and a realist in his own right was William Dean Howells, who adapted English realism to an American audience, including in his novels a good deal of Dickensian "philosophy," that is, observations on human nature.

In these three examples there is seen a development common to any idea, namely, an increase in the difficulty of definition in direct proportion to the age of the idea. But it is important to have these three narrow ideas of realism in mind, since realism, more than any other critical term, is subject to generalization. "All writers believe they are realists," says novelist Alain Robbe-Grillet, and Wendy Lesser reminds us that "the claim made by Symbolists, Expressionists, Modernists, Post-Modernists, and others of this ilk is that their (latest) technique actually presents reality *more* accurately than the previous convention-ridden mode. The term 'realism' has thus taken on the very opposite of its original meaning: it now refers to the strait-jacket imposed on an unruly reality by unimaginative old-timers and their outdated fictional conventions."

A characteristic of any form of realism is that it offers what Claude Lévi-Strauss calls an alternative world of objective reality, another place where we can go whenever we grow weary of this one. A character in Italo Calvino's *If on a Winter's Night a Traveler* says, "I prefer novels that bring me immediately into a world where everything is precise, concrete, specific. I feel a special satisfaction in knowing that things are made in that certain fashion and not otherwise, even the most commonplace things that in real life seem indifferent to me." Perhaps it is this fascination with the commonplace—what a character puts on in the morning, what she eats for breakfast, how she gets to work—that is evoked by poet Galway Kinnell when he writes about an imaginary poem that is "the dream / of all poems and the text / of all loves," a poem called " 'Tenderness Toward Existence.' "

See LOCAL COLOR, MAGIC REALISM, and SURREALISM. For a philosophical definition of realism, see NOMINALISM.

**reality principle**   This principle, which governs the functioning of the EGO, opposes the PLEASURE PRINCIPLE. The reality principle's chief function is to delay gratification until the pleasure that is desired can be achieved in a manner that is the safest, easiest, and most economical as well as the most acceptable to oneself and one's peers.

**red giant**   See STELLAR EVOLUTION.

**red shift**   The increase in wavelength (toward the red or longer-wavelength end of the spectrum) of light from distant galaxies and thus the main evidence for an expanding universe. This type of red shift is a Doppler effect, in which wavelength increases as the distance between source and observer becomes greater and decreases as that distance becomes less. See HUBBLE'S LAW.

Another kind of red shift occurs in accordance with the general theory of RELATIVITY. Since gravity can slow light emissions, the frequency of light emitted by a giant star will be slowed and thus shifted toward the red end of the spectrum. (Since wave frequency and wavelength are inversely proportional, a slower frequency means a longer wavelength.)

***reductio ad absurdum***   The disproof of a proposition by showing that it can be reduced to an absurdity. G. H. Hardy gives as an example Euclid's proof of the existence of an infinity of prime numbers. A prime number can only be divided by itself and 1; thus the numbers 2, 3, 5, 7, 11, 13, 17, 19, 23, 29, etc. are primes. Any number that is not prime may be divided by at least one prime and usually more; for example, 666 may be divided by the primes 2, 3, and 37. If we wanted to prove that there were an infinity of primes, we could propose a complete series of primes 2, 3, 5 . . . P in which P is the largest prime. But given the formula $Q = (2 \times 3 \times 5 \times \ldots P) + 1$, we see that the number Q is not divisible by $2 \times 3 \times 5 \times \ldots$ P or any part thereof because the remainder 1 will always be left over. Thus Q is not prime. But if it is not prime, then it is divisible by some prime and necessarily a prime that is outside of the series. So the proposition that P is the largest prime and therefore there is a finite number of primes has been reduced to an absurdity. See also GOOGOL and ZENO'S PARADOXES.

***regionalism***   See LOCAL COLOR.

***regression***   A statistical technique involving the dependence of one variable upon another (compare with CORRELATION). For example, there is a regression of blood pressure upon age; if experimenters could add ten years to a subject's age overnight, they would expect to see an increase in the subject's average blood pressure.

**relativism**   The view that beliefs, practices, and occurrences are valid only in context rather than universally. "In everyday life," says Jacques Barzun, "relativism is a familiar adjustment to varied circumstances. It is the flexibility that enables us to understand how a large woman can sit in a small car or a tall man be too short to touch the ceiling." But relativism can be dangerous when one is between cultures. According to Barzun, "There is an ancient tale of a traveler who lost his way and was given shelter by peasants in an isolated hut. As they watched over him they noticed that first he blew on his hands to warm them and later on his soup to cool it. Greatly frightened, in the night they killed him—a dangerous relativist."

**relativity**   Like the quantum theory, Einstein's theory of relativity takes us far from Newton's concept of a simple, three-dimensional, mechanistic universe. Too, as with the photons and electrons of the quantum phyicists, the universe of Einstein cannot be visualized, although it can be described by a rather complex mathematics. When physicist Sir Arthur Eddington was asked in the 1920s if it were true that only three people in the world understood Einstein's theory, he is said to have replied, "Who is the third?"

The idea of relativity in physics is not new. Lincoln Barnett finds in Locke's essay *On Human Understanding* (1690) a simple and still-useful illustration of the concept: "A company of chessmen standing on the same squares of the chessboard where we left them, we say, are all in the same place or unmoved: though perhaps the chessboard has been in the meantime carried out of one room into another. . . . The chessboard, we also say, is in the same place if it remain in the same part of the cabin, though perhaps the ship which it is in sails all the while; and the ship is said to be in the same place supposing it kept the same distance with the neighboring land, though perhaps the earth has turned around; and so chessmen and board and ship have every one changed place in respect to remoter bodies." In the special or restricted theory of relativity (1905), Einstein extended this earthbound metaphor so that it describes the whole universe. By affirming the results of the celebrated Michelson-Morley experiment, which proved the constancy of the speed of light, Einstein proved that only the laws of nature are immutable and that there can be no manmade frame of reference that is absolute. All the elements of the universe are in constant motion, but the motion can be described only in terms of the motion of one body relative to another, because there are no directions and boundaries in space and therefore no fixed frame of reference.

And if the concept of absolute space is meaningless, so is that of absolute time. The uselessness of such an idea as "the present" is illustrated by Barnett via a hypothetical radio communication with the star Arcturus. To contact Arcturus "at present" poses insurmountable difficulties, since it would take thirty-eight years for our message to reach the star and another thirty-eight years for a reply to arrive here on earth. Moreover, since the image we receive of Arcturus consists of light rays that left the star thirty-eight years ago (the figure is the same because light waves and radio waves travel at the same speed), the news we get "at present" may be totally inconsistent with the facts by the time it arrives— in fact, Arcturus may have ceased to exist despite strong radio and optical indications of its existence, and we would be none the wiser for thirty-eight years, because our "present" and the Arcturian "present" are relative, having meaning only within their separate contexts and not in relation to some absolute frame of reference.

If the special theory of relativity changes traditional concepts of space and time, it has a similar effect on the concept of mass. During his work on relativity, Einstein discovered that the mass of an object increased as its speed increased. Further, at some point mass can be converted into energy. Possibly the most famous formula in history is $E = mc^2$, in which $E$ is energy, $m$ is mass, and $c$ is the speed of light. Since $c^2$ (or the speed of light squared) is an enormous number, it follows that the conversion of even a very small amount of mass would yield an extraordinary quantity of energy. If all of the energy in a single gram of material could be released, for example, enough energy would be generated to light 10 million 100-watt light bulbs for an entire day.

The general theory of relativity (1915) extends the special theory to include gravity. What Einstein postulated was that gravity "bent" space and time, making of the universe a gigantic sphere that curved back on itself. Regular Euclidean three-dimensional geometry is useless in describing the universe as seen this way, which is why Einstein spoke of the universe as a four-dimensional space-time continuum. Even in our own world, which we see primarily as a three-dimensional spatial continuum, Einstein's phrase has relevance. Barnett gives the example of an airplane flight from New York to Los Angeles. To the pilot and to the air controllers who are tracking the flight, latitude, longitude, and altitude are meaningless without a fourth coordinate, that of time. Nor do the four coordinates together give an accurate sense of the flight unless they are seen as constantly changing relative to what they were and what they will be. "If one wishes to envisage the flight as a whole, as a physical reality, it cannot be broken down into a series of disconnected take-offs, climbs, guides, and landings. Instead it must be thought of as a continuous curve in a four-dimensional space-time continuum." (In this respect, see HOLISM.) If we extend this homely example to the universe as a whole and bear in mind the relativity of space and time as set forth in the special theory, we get an idea of what Michael H. Hart calls "the most beautiful, elegant, powerful, and intellectually satisfying of all scientific theories." See GEDANKEN EXPERIMENT and RED SHIFT.

**repetition-compulsion**   The realization that everyone has a tendency to repeat certain experiences, even (perhaps especially) unpleasant ones, occupied Freud during his late career. In *Beyond the Pleasure Principle*, he ponders the variety of people whose human relationships all have identical patterns: the benefactor who is abandoned repeatedly by each of her protégés, no matter how different they may be; the lover whose affairs with women are always the same and always end the same; and so on. Freud refers to this "eternal recurrence of the same" (or *ewige Wiederkehr des Gleichen*—the phrase is Nietzsche's) as he marvels over not only these instances of active repetition but also the apparently passive instances, such as the case of a woman who married three times, only to see her husband quickly sicken and die in each case. Further, Freud cites the penetration of the repetition compulsion into the realm of myth and art as he discusses Tasso's *Jerusalem Delivered*. Tasso's hero, Tancred, unwittingly kills his beloved Clorinda when she is disguised as an enemy knight. Later he panics in a magic forest and slashes at a tree with his sword, only to see blood stream from the cut and hear the voice of Clorinda, whose soul is imprisoned in the tree and who berates Tancred for killing her again.

According to Freud's fellow psychoanalyst and biographer Ernest Jones, Freud saw that the repetition-compulsion bespoke the desire to restore a previous state of affairs and that, moreover, the fundamental aim of all instincts is regression, a return to a previous state. The ultimate previous state is the pre-vital, inorganic one; thus it is from the repetition-compulsion that Freud developed his concept of the death instinct. The death instinct is balanced by the life or sexual instinct (*eros*), but nothing is ever that neat in the unconscious mind: to repeat forms of sexual behavior over and over is to subscribe to the death instinct because it shows the desire for regression, yet clearly the creation of new life is a denial of the death instinct.

Norman O. Brown, Freud's latter-day interpreter, translates the death instinct from an individual to a cosmic scale when he writes: "Mankind today is still making history without having any conscious idea of what it really wants or under what conditions it would stop being unhappy; in fact what it is doing seems to be making itself more unhappy and calling that unhappiness progress. . . . Freud was right: our real desires are unconscious. It also begins to be apparent that mankind, unconscious of its real desires and therefore unable to obtain satisfaction, is hostile to life and ready to destroy itself. Freud was right in positing a death instinct, and the development of weapons of destruction makes our present dilemma plain: we either come to terms with our unconscious instincts and drives—with life and with death—or else we surely die."

**repression**  A defense mechanism whereby one keeps unacceptable ideas or impulses from entering the conscious mind. Early in his practice Freud noticed an unmistakable avoidance on the part of his patients of memories that were unpleasant to them. Ernest Jones, Freud's biographer, notes that "it could not have been difficult to surmise that the roundabout meanderings were an expression of this resistance, an attempt to postpone the emergence of the significant memory, and yet they followed a route ultimately connected with it. This would justify his patience in following the trains of thought with the closest attention and in the greatest detail."

**restituting tendency** The tendency to compensate for real or imagined wrongs. When Freud was a child, he promised his mother that he would buy her a chair to replace one he had soiled with his dirty hands; he also told his father he would buy "a beautiful new red bed" to take the place of the one he wet at night. These are examples of the restituting tendency and proof, says Freud's biographer Ernest Jones, that "love is stronger than aggression."

**rococo** An artistic style that flourished mainly in the eighteenth century and that is marked by a gay, ornamental playfulness; sometimes used as a pejorative to mean a decadent phase of the BAROQUE movement.

**romanticism** In its ideal form, the unshackling of the imagination and the realization of the power to invoke, in Shelley's words, "light and fire from those eternal regions where the owl-winged faculty of calculation dare not ever soar." In its degenerate form, loss of reason. "Tigers are more beautiful than sheep," wrote Bertrand Russell, "but we prefer them behind bars. The typical romantic removes the bars and enjoys the magnificent leaps with which the tiger annihilates the sheep. He exhorts men to imagine themselves tigers, and when he succeeds the results are not wholly pleasant." Hitler said he would kill reason; according to F. L. Lucas, he boasted of "marching to his goal like a somnambulist, and intoxicated both himself and his countrymen with megalomaniac dreams."

As a movement in the arts in the late eighteenth and early nineteenth centuries, romanticism is associated with a variety of themes. No single work contains all of them, but any romantic poem or painting will treat some combination of the following: emotionalism, mysticism, individualism, introspection, morbid melancholy, primitivism (the cult of the "noble savage" untouched by science and reason), a celebration of natural beauty and the simple life, an idealization of the common man, an interest in the picturesque past and in remote places.

These new aesthetic emphases were but part of a worldwide revolution in politics, religion, economics, manners, and morals; however, the rebellion against Shelley's "owl-winged faculty of calculation" gave rise to a variety of romanticisms. For example, Jack D. Zipes reminds us that the German romantic writers and philosophers who provided the impetus for English and American romanticism represented an urban and cosmopolitan viewpoint that sought the *refinement* of a preexisting culture, whereas the provincial American romantics espoused a largely Rousseauistic attitude intended to serve as the basis for the *establishment* of a genuine culture. Differences aside, both of these romanticisms have a common starting point; both are reactions against the strictures of eighteenth-century CLASSICISM. In turn, the excesses of romanticism are at least partly responsible for the mid-nineteenth-century turn toward REALISM.

**Rorshach test**   A type of PROJECTIVE TEST designed by Swiss psychiatrist Hermann Rorshach in which ten standardized inkblots are interpreted by subjects in ways that project personality characteristics. Since the blots are ambiguous, there is no right or wrong response to them; rather, the subject will reveal unresolved conflicts simply through reactions to the test.

# S

**sadism**    Specifically, an abnormality in which sexual pleasure is derived from inflicting physical pain on others; generally, a tendency toward cruelty. Since the sadist establishes selfhood through actions, sadism is the opposite of MASOCHISM, because the masochist wants to undergo a loss of self. The line between opposing tendencies is seldom clear in psychoanalysis, however, and Simone de Beauvoir points out that the masochist may become a sadist by tyrannizing an unwilling partner and insisting on mistreatment.

Too, sadism may serve an ostensibly beneficial purpose. Ernest Jones, Freud's biographer, says that Freud came to see masochism as a self-injuring tendency that sometimes turned to sadism in order to "save life a little longer," much as a ruler might deflect revolutionary impulses by declaring war on another country.

Sadism takes its name from Donatien Alphonse François, Comte de Sade, better known as the Marquis de Sade (he assumed the title of count on his father's death). De Sade was charged with numerous acts of sodomy, flagellation, and so on, and spent most of his adult life in prisons, during which time he wrote *120 Days of Sodom* (finished in 1785 but not published until 1904) and other novels as well as plays and political essays. In the headnote to "Dialogue Between a Priest and a Dying Man," his earliest dated work, De Sade is described as "a minor practitioner of and then a major writer about extreme sexuality"; he saw himself and is seen by others as one who was more revolutionary than criminal, an advanced thinker who wanted to revive primitive impulses in a tired and overrefined world.

**sadomasochism**   See SADISM and MASOCHISM.


**Sapir-Whorf hypothesis**   This linguistic and anthropological hypothesis developed by Edward Sapir and Benjamin Lee Whorf says that our view of the world is partly determined by our native language. Thus dwellers in moderate climes see only "snow" in the winter (if at all) and use a single word to describe it, whereas Eskimos see a variety of types of snow and have a different word for each. This aspect of their world is more complex than ours not because their weather is different but because the Eskimos have developed this part of their language more than we have.


**satire**   A form of imitation in which criticism and humor coexist; ridicule with the intent to improve. An example is Jonathan Swift's "A Modest Proposal." Superfically a serious treatise on the problem of poverty in Ireland, Swift's essay reveals itself to be an assault on heartless English landlords who might actually permit Irish children to be sold and eaten. See PARODY for a distinction between that form and satire.


**schizophrenia**   A form of PSYCHOSIS in which there is dissociation between intellectual and emotional processes; literally "split-mindedness." The schizophrenic may drive a car, buy groceries, and even hold down a job while at the same time suffering from a wide and shifting range of symptoms, including hallucinations, inconsistent behavior, and loss of contact with the environment. Sleep researchers theorize that schizophrenics may actually dream while they are awake: they seldom experience rapid-eye-movement or REM sleep, the sleep that characterizes the dream state, so they may do their dreaming while awake and conclude that, since they are not asleep, their dreams must be real.

In the more specialized case of paranoid schizophrenia, the individual suffers from persistent and unchanging hallucinations and is not likely to experience the full spectrum of symptoms seen in ordinary schizophrenics. Paranoid schizophrenia is of paramount importance to legal defenses based on insanity, many of which invoke the so-called M'Naghten Rule. Daniel M'Naghten believed that Sir Robert Peel, the prime minister of England, was conspiring against him, and on January 20, 1843, M'Naghten shot to death a man whom he thought was Peel but was actually Edward Drummond, the prime minister's private secretary. M'Naghten was acquitted of the crime because he was found to be legally insane—not because he could not tell right from wrong, which is a popular misconception of the M'Naghten Rule, but because his crime was the logical consequence of an illogical premise.

Psychiatrist Donald T. Lunde frequently serves as a consultant in capital cases and he distinguishes very carefully between different types of murderers. For example, a mass murderer named Herbert Mullin heard voices that told him that the deaths he caused would prevent earthquakes and other natural disasters. A classic paranoid schizophrenic like M'Naghten, Mullin had a crazy theory that dictated an action that would have made sense had the theory made sense; the job of the defense in a case like this is to prove that the accused held such a theory long before any crime was committed and was not simply thinking up excuses after the fact. In contrast, a second mass murderer, Ed Kemper, who killed and dissected young women (as Mullin did in at least one case), was not legally insane. While it is easy to say that anyone would have to be insane to commit such crimes, the point is that Kemper was not a paranoid schizophrenic like Mullin but a sexual sadist who did what he did for no other reason than the fact that he wanted to.

**scholasticism**   The term assigned to the philosophy and theology (usually considered inseparable) of Western Christendom between roughly the ninth and the seventeenth centuries. Building on a foundation of NEOPLATONISM, scholasticism was enriched by the introduction of Aristotle's ideas by the two Arabic commentators Avicenna and Averroës and, especially, by the philosophical writings of St. Thomas Aquinas.

Ironically, because the originally powerful philosophy of the major schoolmen became mere verbalism in the hands of their followers, scholasticism is sometimes used pejoratively to mean something like ALEXANDRIANISM or, as Jacques Barzun says, "the Byzantine magnification of trifles" ("its very name still retains the connotation of decline to futility").

**screen memory**   An unimportant memory that takes the place of an important one; also called a cover memory. Freud had a Czech nannie, an old and ugly woman to whom he remembers giving all his pennies. Freud cites this as an example of a screen memory, since he apparently substituted this memory of his childish generosity for a more important occurrence, namely, that the old woman had been dismissed for theft.

A more recent example occurs in the murder of Herman Tarnower, the so-called "Scarsdale diet doctor," by his cast-off lover, Jean Harris. At her trial, Harris seemed undisturbed by the death of Tarnower, though she recalled with horror her initial stay in jail, when, according to her testimony, the prostitutes she had been put among threw their bloody sanitary pads on the cell floor. Even assuming that most or all of Mrs. Harris's cellmates were menstruating prostitutes, it seems likely that instead of *throwing* their pads on the floor they simply *put* them there for lack of anyplace else. Thus Diana Trilling is correct when she says "this may have been a cover memory for a suppressed recollection of the blood that had been spilled in Dr. Tarnower's bedroom."

**semiology**   The science of signs; how we communicate via language as well as gestures, music, choice of food and clothes, and so on. Semiology is based on the work of Swiss linguist Ferdinand de Saussure, who argued the relational nature of language, and was later developed by French literary critic Roland Barthes. According to Saussure, any element of a linguistic system (any *parole* or "word") exists only in terms of the speaker's overall knowledge of the system (the *langue* or "language"). Thus words are arbitrary signs—"dog" refers to a certain animal, but there is nothing in "dog" itself to make this so. As for applying semiology to broader cultural phenomena, consider this description by novelist Edith Wharton of the highly stylized New York society from which she came: "They all lived in a kind of hieroglyphic world, where the real thing was never said or done or even thought, but only represented by a set of arbitrary signs."

As with late nineteenth- and early twentieth-century developments in other fields (see IMPRESSIONISM and QUANTUM MECHANICS, for example), Saussurian linguistics emphasizes not an objective external reality but an interplay between perceiver and perceived. Similarly, there is a tendency in semiology as in other aspects of MODERNISM toward the recondite and obscure. See STRUCTURALISM.

**semiotics**  When the broad concerns of SEMIOLOGY are restricted to the study of patterned human communication only, the term "semiotics" is generally preferred.

**set theory**  No less than "the foundation stone of the edifice of modern mathematics," according to *The Van Nostrand Reinhold Concise Encyclopedia of Mathematics*, set theory is born of the application of SYMBOLIC LOGIC to sets of numbers by German mathematician Georg Cantor. A set is a collection of like members, e.g., Ms. Ferrell's fourth-grade class, or all of the alligators in the world. There are a variety of types of sets, including empty or null sets, which contain no members, and subsets, or sets contained in other sets—"all of the alligators in Florida" is a subset of "all of the alligators in the world." Mathematical operations involving the manipulation of sets unite arithmetic, algebra, and geometry with such branches of higher mathematics as topology (see under MÖBIUS STRIP), which is heavily dependent on set theory. In logic, set theory underlies the function of the SYLLOGISM—if all of the children in Ms. Ferrell's fourth-grade class play soccer, and William is a member of Ms. Ferrell's fourth-grade class, then William plays soccer.

**singularity**  The point at which a physical law breaks down. In *A Comprehensible World*, Jeremy Bernstein notes that "very often what singularities have meant is that . . . laws are being extrapolated to places where they no longer apply. Historically, singularities are often the symptoms of a sick theory, and in many cases the cure has turned out to be an entirely new physics." A good example of a singularity can be found at the center of a black hole. There, says Eliot Fremont-Smith, is "that point or line at which all things, all mass, all energy, all information, are infinitely impacted, fused, and stopped. Or made entirely chaotic. It is in the nature of a singularity that definitions of 'cause,' 'time,' 'chaos,' etc., along with discernible laws of nature, cease to have meaning." See BLACK HOLE; see also BAYES'S THEOREM.


**social contract**    The implicit agreement between members of a society to surrender some individual governance in order to unite for mutual protection. The idea is as old as Plato, though modern interpretations of it derive chiefly from the work of Thomas Hobbes, Jean-Jacques Rousseau, who devoted a celebrated book to the subject, and John Locke, who achieved a certain popularity among the American revolutionaries because he argued that since moral principles preexisted any state, the state could be changed if it ceased to adhere to those principles.


**social realism**    An artistic style that arose in the United States in the 1930s, social realism was concerned primarily with the injustices suffered by the poor and the working class. It is an angry and political style; David Shapiro's book on the subject is called *Social Realism: Art as a Weapon*. A representative of the movement is Ben Shahn, who treated the Sacco-Vanzetti trial in a series of twenty-three paintings called *The Passion of Sacco and Vanzetti*.


**socialist realism**    Not to be confused with SOCIAL REALISM, socialist realism is an artistic mode that uses the techniques of REALISM to promote a positive image of Russian life; it was announced at the 1934 Soviet Writers' Congress by Maxim Gorky and others. Denounced by Westerners and dissident Russians as stifling, this same approach has significantly affected the

arts in China in this century. See also CONSTRUCTIVISM and
FORMALISM.


***sociobiology***   In *Sociobiology: The New Synthesis*, Edward
O. Wilson advanced the belief that the behavior of humans, like
that of all animals, is significantly predetermined by genetic
forces beyond our control, that our "selfish" genes are responsible
not only for much of the mayhem in our lives but also the qualities
we prize as most human, from the altruism of the soldier who lays
down his life so that his comrades may live and perpetuate the
species to the apparently unlearned smile of the infant who is encouraging her parents to nurture her.

Before this book, sociobiology was somewhat faddish in nature;
after its publication, the views of Wilson and his followers became
increasingly influential and controversial, as racial, political, and
sexist messages were read into sociobiological arguments. Not
only is the implicit DETERMINISM of sociobiology objectionable
to many, but so is the reversal of such hard-won victories as the
feminist assertion of identical sexual feelings in men and women.
If the feminists who maintain this are correct, then typically pro-
miscuous males are immoral and uncaring creatures who have
consciously chosen bad behavior over good. But sociobiologists argue that whereas females can best ensure the transmission of
their genes through the monogamy and fidelity that will allow
them to bring a limited number of offspring to maturity, the males
of any species are programmed to pass on their genes through the
insemination of a variety of partners. To illustrate this idea,
sociobiologists sometimes refer to a phenomenon called the
Coolidge Effect, which involves the renewal of male arousal as the
variety of female partners increases. Supposedly President and
Mrs. Coolidge were touring a government chicken farm; when the
President's wife was told that each of the roosters copulated dozens of times a day, she said to her guide, "Please tell that to the
President." When he was told, Coolidge asked if the rooster fre-
quented the same hen every time; learning that the rooster al-
ways had a new partner, Coolidge replied, "Well, tell *that* to Mrs.
Coolidge."

Biology is neither moral nor immoral, say sociobiologists. Our instinctive genetic drives are like gravity or any other natural force: knowing about them will not make them go away, but it will allow us to devise strategies that will compensate for them.

**solar system**   A SYSTEM of planets and other bodies (asteroids, meteoroids, etc.) that are attracted to and revolve around a sun. See GALAXY.

**solecism**   Specifically, a solecism is a grammatical error, such as "Dad loves Ian and I"; generally, the term refers to any impropriety or incongruity in speech or writing.

**solipsism**   Philosophical belief in the self alone; other entities may appear to exist, but they do so only in one's own consciousness. The opposite of OBJECTIVISM.

**space-time**   See RELATIVITY.

**split-brain analysis**   Study of the two brain hemispheres. The left hemisphere governs analytic abilities and concerns itself with problems in logic, whereas the right hemisphere is the seat of intuition and nonverbal perception. The left hemisphere deals with structural approaches, such as the SYLLOGISM, whereas the right hemisphere handles images and is responsible for GE-STALT perceptions. Somewhat confusingly, the rational left hemisphere governs the right side of the body, whereas the dreamy right hemisphere controls the side that is "sinister" (French *sinistre* or "left") and accounts for a longlived suspicion of the left-handed.

One of the most controversial uses of split-brain analysis resulted in Julian Jaynes's book *The Origin of Consciousness in the Breakdown of the Bicameral Mind*. In this provocative amalgam of biology, anthropology, psychology, history, linguistics, and literary criticism, Jaynes argues that before the year 2000 B.C., there was no consciousness as we know it today. What happened was that the dreamy right brain muttered to the wide-awake left brain via a nerve pathway called the anterior commissure; naturally enough, it seemed to the left brain that it was hearing voices that were coming from outside the body. In books like the *Iliad*, then, gods took the place of consciousness, and, indeed, it is common in Homer's epic to have some character receive a directive from a god, only to turn and find no one there. Jaynes has prompted a fellow psychologist named Ronald Hayes to state that if the bicameral theory were true, then "the Code of Hammurabi and large portions of the Old Testament are products of people who today would be shuffling through mental institutions."

**steady-state theory** See BIG-BANG THEORY.

**stellar evolution** By plotting two observable characteristics of stars (surface temperature and absolute brightness) on a graph called the Hertzsprung-Russell diagram, astrophysicists are able to determine the evolutionary stage that a star has reached at the time of observation. Most stars lie along a band on the graph called the main sequence, where our own sun is located. A star spends much of its life evolving toward or along the main sequence, deriving its energy from the burning of hydrogen in the stellar core. When the resultant ashes catch fire, the star expands and becomes a red giant (a star of low density that is relatively cool though very luminous because of its great size, like Betelgeuse and Antares). A star like our sun then shrinks until it becomes a white dwarf (a dense white-hot star with a feeble glow) before burning out. A nova occurs when a shrinking star sheds its outer mantle. Stars can survive one or several such outbursts. In contrast, a supernova is the result of a single explosion, after which there is an expanding cloud of debris and a dense stellar remnant that has contracted beyond the white-dwarf stage into a neutron star or pulsar. The ultimate stage of contraction, of course, is the BLACK HOLE.

**stochastic process** Any process governed by the laws of probability (see PROBABILITY THEORY).

**stream of consciousness**  First used by psychologist and philosopher William James, this phrase refers to the total flood of mental and emotional experience, from the skimpiest VELLEITY to the most carefully articulated idea. Implicit in this concept is Freud's idea of different psychological levels and the constant tension between ID, EGO, and SUPEREGO. The first use of the stream of consciousness as a literary technique occurs in Edouard Dujardin's *Les Lauriers Sont Coupés* (1888); a celebrated twentieth-century example is Molly Bloom's interior monologue at the close of James Joyce's *Ulysses* (1922). See DURATION.


**structuralism**  An analytical method in anthropology introduced by Claude Lévi-Strauss and now used in literary criticism as well. Both the anthropological and the literary varieties of structuralism are rooted in the Saussurian linguistics that is the basis of SEMIOLOGY; both assume that cultural phenomena are languages, systems of relations, codes derived from the innate structuring tendency of the mind, whether collective (as in the case of a tribal group, be it primitive hill people or high-fashion models) or individual (such as the poet or novelist who is in effect writing the same work over and over again). An analysis based on the idea that these codes are important not for their contents but for their structures is intended to reveal the unconscious but consistent laws that govern any phenomenon.

   Some of those who see the virtue of the structuralist approach see certain drawbacks in it as well. Reviewing David Lodge's *Working with Structuralism: Essays and Reviews on Nineteenth- and Twentieth-Century Literature*, Graham Hough observes that Lodge "gives the impression of being able to screw himself up to a structuralist stance, and to enjoy it for a time; but after a bit he begins to relax and slip back into the old ways, to talk about a novel as if it were a representation of a particular social world, its characters as if they were acting and suffering human beings. And that I think points to the inherent limitation of structuralist criticism. It is strenuous, it is active, it does much of what the old Anglo-American New Criticism did and puts it on a far firmer intellectual foundation. But it is fatally remote from the way in which literature is ordinarily discussed. It is useless as an educational foundation for young students with no stock of reading or literary experience behind them. It remains among the dogmatisms of learning. And even esoteric criticism depends for its survival on the ability to take its place in the ordinary conversation of mankind." As Aristotle is reputed to have said, there is nothing in the intellect that was not first in the senses.

Some authorities treat SEMIOLOGY as though it were interchangeable with structuralism; too, there are important connections between structuralism and PHENOMENOLOGY. (Jonathan Culler says that "the phenomenologist becomes a structuralist if he considers the implication of his method, and . . . the structuralist must become a phenomenologist if he scrutinizes the foundation of his method.") See also DECONSTRUCTION, which has to some extent succeeded structuralism as a literary approach. And while these competing -isms and -ologies may sometimes appear to be merely the last word in academic overrefinement, their effect in the world is palpable nonetheless; David Walker reports that the debate over structuralism in the literature departments of English universities has prompted faculty resignations at Cambridge and allegations of antistructuralist bias in the grading of examinations at Oxford.

**subconscious**   A popular term that refers to processes that take place beneath the workings of the CONSCIOUS. However, this term fails to distinguish between the Freudian ideas of the preconscious, the state of mind characterized by thoughts that can be made conscious by ordinary efforts at recall, and the UNCONSCIOUS, the state that can be illuminated only through some therapy, such as psychoanalysis.

**subtext**   In literature, particularly the drama, subtext refers to the private knowledge and feelings that a character has and that underlie that character's public behavior. An effective example of the interaction between text and subtext is *Hamlet*, where the other characters are baffled by the strange actions and statements that are prompted by Hamlet's secret knowledge of his father's murder.

**superego**  The strict and moralistic aspect of the mind; the censor. The superego's function is largely unconscious, though it manifests itself consciously in the form of shame and guilt. Typically, criminals do not have highly developed superegos.

Neither, according to Freud, do women. Janet Malcolm quotes a 1925 Freud essay entitled "Some Psychical Consequences of the Anatomical Distinction Between the Sexes": "I cannot evade the notion (though I hesitate to give it expression) that for women the level of what is ethically normal is different from what it is in men. . . . Their superego is never so inexorable, so impersonal, so independent of its emotional origins as we require it to be in men. Character traits which critics of every epoch have brought up against women—that they show less sense of justice than men, that they are less ready to submit to the great exigencies of life, that they are more often influenced in their judgments by feelings of affection or hostility—all these would be amply accounted for by the modification in the formation of their superego which we have inferred above." This formation of the superego to which Freud refers is quite different for the two sexes. In both cases the superego is born of the Oedipus/Electra conflict, in which the child develops feelings of love for the parent of the opposite sex and feelings of jealousy toward the parent of the same sex. Whereas the female child foresees no very harsh consequences of such feelings, the male child develops a castration anxiety stimulated by fears that his father will punish his incestuous sexual longings brutally and maimingly. As Malcolm says, " 'The little lover' of four or five gives up his ambitions toward his mother *fast*, and forever." But he retains his fear of punishment; as a consequence, says Freud, the male is more moral than the female.

Recent psychological theory has not so much denied Freud's view as expanded it to include points that Freud did not or would not make. The stereotypically rigid male viewpoint has its evident and often ironic drawbacks; witness the conflicted characters of so many "great men," such as Rousseau, who ruthlessly consigned his children to a foundling home so that he could write undisturbed on the ideal schooling of children, among other topics. Carol Gilligan writes scathingly of Mahatma Gandhi, virtually a saint to an admiring world yet a psychologically destructive and emotionally distant man to his wife, children, and disciples. Gandhi had "a blind willingness to sacrifice people to truth," says

Gilligan. "This willingness links Gandhi to the biblical Abraham, who prepared to sacrifice the life of his son in order to demonstrate the integrity and supremacy of his faith. Both men, in the limitations of their fatherhood, stand in implicit contrast to the woman who comes before Solomon and verifies her motherhood by relinquishing truth in order to save the life of her child."

For better or worse, there are few men with superegos as ferocious as Rousseau's or Gandhi's, just as there are few "pure" men or women of any kind. In his essay quoted above, Freud observed that "all human individuals, as a result of their bisexual disposition and of cross-inheritance, combine in themselves both masculine and feminine characteristics, so that pure masculinity and femininity remain theoretical constructs of uncertain content." See EGO and ID.


**supernova**    See STELLAR EVOLUTION.


**surrealism**    An arts movement whose works represent the breakthrough of dreams into the world of waking reality. Given its impetus by André Breton in his "Manifeste du Surréalisme" (1924) and characterized in its early days by experiments in automatic writing and drawing and other methods of evoking unconscious images, surrealism clearly owes much to DADA, though, as Craig Adcock observes, "the transition from Dada to Surrealism involved a theoretical shift from destruction to construction." Surrealism's true spiritual ancestors include Arthur Rimbaud, Charles Baudelaire, and other practitioners of ROMANTICISM and SYMBOLISM.

There is nothing abstract about the surreal, since its images are the hard-edged objects of everyday life, even though they are placed in startling juxtaposition to one another. Jean-Pierre Cauvin says that "Breton is keenly aware of Freud's discovery that, in dreams, the categories of contradiction and opposition are voided, that the unconscious is blind to negation, and that dreams evince a particular tendency to join opposites together into a unit or to represent them in a single object. . . . Characterized by immediacy and incongruence, surrealist images bypass all willful intellectual controls."

Typical of the surrealists in the visual arts are René Magritte, whose most widely reproduced painting, *Le Fils d'Homme* (1964), shows a man whose face is obscured by a large green apple that seems to be floating in space, and Giorgio de Chirico, with his empty and somehow vaguely meancing urban landscapes. The effect of de Chirico's paintings is dreamlike; as in a dream, the images are both disturbing and real, perhaps the more disturbing precisely because they are real. Of de Chirico's work John Russell Taylor notes that "it does not come from nothing. . . . Anyone who has ever arrived in some strange Italian town in the early afternoon must have had the feeling of having wandered into a de Chirico painting." See ULTRAISM.

**syllogism**    A logical formula consisting of three propositions: the major premise, containing the major term; the minor premise, containing the minor term; and the conclusion, which links the two terms.

> Major premise: All fish are animals. (Major term: animals.)
> Minor premise: All trout are fish. (Minor term: trout.)
> Conclusion: Therefore, all trout are animals.

The major and minor premise must have a middle term in common that makes a logical connection between them and leads to the joining of the major and minor terms in the conclusion, even though it is not stated there; in this case, the middle term is "fish." Failure to make this logical connection results in something called the fallacy of the undistributed middle term, as in this example: "All fish can swim; all snakes can swim; therefore all fish are snakes." This fallacy is often behind half-baked political assumptions, e.g., "All communist countries ban handguns; this particular group of American citizens supports the banning of handguns; therefore this particular group is communist."

**symbol**    An image is a concrete representation of an experience or an object; if there is a secondary meaning behind the concrete one, then the image becomes a symbol. Thus, in a film, a man cutting someone's throat does not symbolize violence; it *is* violence, or, to be more precise, it is an image of violence. In this case, there is only one meaning. But a symbol always has two meanings. For example, a woman who makes the sign of the cross is doing something concrete (moving her hand in a stylized fashion), but she is also evoking an invisible event (Christ's sacrifice); therefore hers is a symbolic gesture.

Symbols are of two types: public (the cross, a country's flag) and private (a dancer's rhythmic patterns, an obscure figure in a painting). Only an adherent of POSITIVISM would fail to see the true nature of a public symbol, but private symbols clearly allow for a variety of interpretations. Of course many artists count on the reader's ability to give a private symbol the meaning that the artist intends. An example can be found in Richard Wilbur's poem "Love Calls Us to the Things of This World" (1956), where laundry represents the human condition, now spotless and angelic, now stained. In this case, the symbol seems to arise naturally from the poet's desire to make a certain statement. Such a symbol is quite different from, say, the highly artificial conceits of the seventeenth-century metaphysical poets, such as the celebrated compass that represents the two lovers in John Donne's "A Valediction: Forbidding Mourning" (c1611). Admirable in its own right, Donne's compass is an example of the poet's ingenuity rather than a deeply expressive symbol of an impersonal theme.

Regardless of the use to which symbols are put, the symbols must follow in order of importance the narrative itself and not vice versa. Mary McCarthy warns that "outlines, patterns, arrangements of symbols may have a certain usefulness at the outset for some kinds of minds, but in the end they will have to be scrapped. If the story does not contradict the outline, overrun the pattern, break the symbols, like an insurrection against authority, it is surely a still birth. The natural symbolism of reality has more messages to communicate than the dry Morse code of the disengaged mind."

Indeed, symbols assume so much importance in psychoanalysis, the arts, and all forms of human expression that it is best to recall that to attribute too much importance to them is a form of insanity. G. K. Chesterton points out the flaw in the old saying "he has

lost his mind" by observing that-the insane person has lost everything but his mind. To the normal person, a man swishing some
weeds with his walking stick is doing little or nothing while to the
disturbed person these gestures betoken a wanton assault on public property, perhaps, or a signal to a hidden accomplice. Not
everything that appears to be a symbol is; as Freud said, sometimes a cigar is just a cigar.

See SYMBOLISM for a discussion of the development of some
of these ideas into a specific movement in the nineteenth century.


**symbolic logic**   Traditional logic replaces words with letters in orer to study logical relationships; e.g., from "No A is B"
infer that "No B is A." Symbolic or mathematical logic uses mathematical symbolism to perform more sophisticated manipulations.
Boolean algebra (developed by nineteenth-century English mathematician George Boole) is an early form of symbolic logic; note
also the influence of symbolic logic on SET THEORY.


**Symbolism**   A romantic reaction to REALISM and NATU-
RALISM, Symbolism brings to the arts the Freudian view that
the commonplace may have mysterious and private implications,
that there is always more than meets the eye. If naturalists like
Zola believed that a novel was a sort of laboratory experiment in
which a character was given a certain heredity and environment
to which he or she responded with automatic reactions, the Symbolists (who, like the naturalists, came to prominence in France
during the latter half of the nineteenth century) argued that man
was the creature who dreamed and that art should reflect our pre-
occupation with the symbols that give life meaning. Charles
Baudelaire, a forerunner of the movement, was much influenced
by the writings of Edgar Allan Poe, as were the Symbolists
Stephane Mallarmé and Paul Valéry, who themselves influenced
such modern masters as W. B. Yeats, James Joyce, and Rainer
Maria Rilke.

So important is the interplay between the naturalist and Sym-
bolist viewpoints that Edmund Wilson has said that the literary

history of our times is largely the story of the dynamic between the two outlooks, their fusion or their failure to fuse. The viewpoints come together in such representative twentieth-century works as Eliot's *The Waste Land* (1922) and Hemingway's *The Sun Also Rises* (1926), both of which have symbolically impotent main characters who represent naturalistic fallen worlds. On the other hand, much lyric poetry describes symbolically worlds that are decidedly nonnaturalistic, just as much popular fiction depicts a seedily naturalistic world that is described with perfect realism, that is, in a nonsymbolic, "nonliterary" way.

See both ROMANTICISM, out of which Symbolism developed, and MODERNISM, on which it had a striking impact.

**synchronicity**   Carl Jung proposed an acausal connecting principle called "synchronicity" (from the Greek "simultaneousness"). His own life abounded with such episodes, as when he experienced the image of someone drowning during a train trip and arrived to find that his grandson had nearly died in the water at about the time that Jung had experienced the image. Jung collaborated in his study of synchronous events with physicist Wolfgang Pauli, and the implications of their work are seen in such concepts as BELL'S THEOREM and the HIDDEN-VARIABLE THEORY.

**synergy**   The creation of a new SYSTEM, presumably with increased benefits, out of a combination of systems.

**system**   An orderly combination of related elements. See CYBERNETICS and SYNERGY.

**systems analysis**   An approach to problem solving that treats each task not as a single entity but as a SYSTEM; also called systems approach. The systems analyst must define the boundaries of the problem and decide which elements are included and which are not. Obviously, systems analysis has broad implications for computer programming and other aspects of ARTIFICIAL INTELLIGENCE.

**systems approach**    See SYSTEMS ANALYSIS.

# T

**tautology**    Generally, a pejorative term that refers to the unnecessary repetition of identical ideas in different words, e.g., "a widow whose husband has died." In logic, however, a tautology is simply a statement that is true because of its form, one that need not be verified (and cannot be falsified) by the senses or through testing, as in "A widow is a woman whose husband has died." It is said that all scientific reasoning is basically tautological in nature when traced through to its roots.

**teleology**    In theology and philosophy, the study of order, design, and purpose. See VITALISM.

**thematic apperception test (TAT)**    A PROJEC-
TIVE TEST designed by American psychologist Henry Murray in which a subject is asked to make up stories about a standardized series of deliberately vague pictures. Convicted killer Tony Costa exhibited certain childlike qualities when he took the TAT, qualities that correlated with the anger that he felt toward a "corrupt" adult world that he tried to punish through his murders. Writing about Costa, Leo Damore noted that the killer's TAT stories usually took place in the course of a single day and ended with the protagonist resolving all conflicts neatly before toddling home to supper and a good night's sleep. Costa also dwelled on sexual activity and seemed unable to restrain his comments in that area; according to the TAT administrator who tested him, Costa's stories

seemed to be those of a little boy "who cannot resist the temptation of peeking into the grown-up world after the other children have gone to bed."

**thermodynamics, laws of**   There are three of these laws concerning the relation of heat to other forms of energy. The first holds that heat may be converted into mechanical work and vice versa, and the third says that at absolute zero temperature a substance would have zero entropy. It is this idea of entropy and its implications for the second law of thermodynamics, however, that have interested so many thinkers, humanists as well as scientists. The second law states that heat will always flow from a hotter substance to a cooler and that therefore every SYSTEM, including the universe, is headed toward an entropic state. At the state of maximum entropy, everything will be at the same temperature; in this condition of "heat death," all fundamental processes will cease, and time itself will end.

The second law of thermodynamics is irreversible; in Lincoln Barrett's words, "nature moves just one way." Ironically, what is true of the inorganic universe seems countered by the processes of evolution, especially human evolution, in which the trend is toward complexity rather than simplicity, toward the vertical rather than the horizontal. (A natural trend, the evolutionary process is being speeded up by geneticists who are attempting to eliminate genetically transmitted disease, stop the aging process, and extend life.) Thus there is a decided rift between our conscious perception of the entropic nature of the universe and our unconscious biological urgings toward the continuance of the race. It is out of this "growing schizophrenia," says Amaury de Riencourt, that "all the philosophical problems of the West have sprung." See MAXWELL'S DEMON.

**three-body problem**   In both QUANTUM MECHANICS and astronomy, the equations that describe the interactions of two bodies become useless when a third body is introduced. Electromagnetic or gravitational pull on all three bodies produces an endless variety of relationships, for example, as John Nuttall writes, a situation in which "one particle remains a spectator while the other two interact." Anyone who has introduced her husband to an old friend, only to note that neither acts as he or she does when alone with her (who may behave differently herself in this new configuration), has an instinctive understanding of the three-body problem.

**topology** See MÖBIUS STRIP and SET THEORY.

**tragedy** In his *Poetics*, Aristotle defined tragedy as the representation of an action that (1) is serious, complete, and of a certain magnitude, (2) involves a tragic hero who goes from a high to a low state because of some fatal flaw in his character, and (3) arouses pity and fear in the audience in order to purge it of these emotions. A classic example is the *Oedipus Rex* of Sophocles.

Generally, "tragedy" has come to refer to any serious drama in which a protagonist of some importance comes to an unhappy end.

**transactional analysis** Developed by American pyschiatrist Eric Berne and popularized in his book *Games People Play*, transactional analysis posits three ego states: parent, adult, and child. Ideally, people should deal with each other on an adult-to-adult level socially and psychologically, but in reality, people play games with each other and with themselves, so that what appears to be one kind of transaction may be another kind altogether. Berne gives the following conversation as an example. "Cowboy: 'Come and see the barn.' Visitor: 'I've loved barns ever since I was a little girl.' . . . At the social level," says Berne, "this is an Adult conversation about barns, and at the psychological level it is a Child conversation about sex play. On the surface the Adult seems to have the initiative, but as in most games, the outcome is determined by the Child, and the participants may be in for a surprise."

Transactional analysis is particularly appropriate for group settings, where the analyst can describe the games patients play with each other and encourage more productive behavior.

**transference**   The feeling in adult life of emotions felt in childhood and stimulated by someone other than the person who stimulated them originally. Transference is the means by which "we all invent each other according to early blueprints," notes Janet Malcolm, who calls transference "Freud's most original and radical discovery." The origin of the idea of transference and thus of psychoanalysis itself lies in Freud's understanding of the work of Austrian physician and physiologist Josef Breuer. In 1880 Breuer treated a twenty-one-year-old woman named Anna O., who suffered from HYSTERIA. Beautiful and intelligent, Anna so engrossed Breuer that he began to talk to his wife only of his young patient, to the exclusion of all other topics. His wife bore Breuer's monomania in patient silence, though secretly she became quite jealous and unhappy. At last realizing the danger to which he was subjecting his marriage, Breuer abruptly terminated the treatment of Anna, who was, at any rate, much improved. But that evening Breuer was called back and found Anna as hysterical as ever. Having struck Breuer as totally asexual throughout the treatment, Anna was now going through a false childbirth, the logical consequence of the false pregnancy that had been subconsciously provoked by Breuer's tender and well-intentioned response to his patient's needs. Shocked, Breuer calmed Anna with hypnosis. The next day, he and his wife went to Venice for a second honeymoon, during which a real child was conceived. (Ernest Jones, Freud's biographer, notes in a haunting sentence that "the girl born in these curious circumstances was nearly sixty years later to commit suicide in New York.")

What had happened was that Anna had developed a strong transference to her therapist, investing in him feelings that he had not elicited but that she had carried over from the normal Electral urgings of her childhood. Freud had similar experiences, of course, and it is in his cool reaction to them (as opposed to Breuer's panic) that we see the difference between mere intellect and genius. In an article entitled "The Therapeutic Revolution: From Mesmer to Freud," French psychoanalysts Léon Chertok and Raymond de Saussure (quoted in Malcolm) point out that Breuer took Anna's behavior personally because he saw himself as an attractive object of her love; consequently he developed a strong countertransference to her. In contrast, Freud had little confidence in his own sexual magnetism. Confronted with the erotic longings of his patients, therefore, Freud cast about for some universal explanation for this untoward conduct, and the result is the principle of transference.

# U

**ultraism**   A Spanish literary movement that flourished in the early 1920s, *ultraísmo* combined elements of SURREALISM and EXPRESSIONISM and advocated the use of bold and original images to create a pure poetry. The term itself was coined by Guillermo de Torre. Jorge Luis Borges is the best-known author to have been influenced by ultraism, even though he was never a strict adherent to its theories.


**uncertainty principle**   In 1927 Werner Heisenberg formulated his uncertainty or indeterminacy principle, which says that it is impossible to determine simultaneously both the position and velocity of a moving electron. Hans Plendl compares the physicist who tries to do this to someone who is trying to determine the position of a moving billiard ball in a dark room; the moment this person touches the ball, he changes its position (by either stopping it or sending it off in a new direction) and affects its velocity as well. Precise measurement is impossible, in other words, for in any act of measurement the observer and the observer's instruments become part of the phenomenon, thus altering it. If you put a thermometer in hot water to measure its temperature, you lower that temperature. Nor will bigger and better thermometers do the trick; Lincoln Barnett explains that indeterminacy "is a symptom not of man's immature science but of an ultimate barrier of nature."

The metaphoric application of the uncertainty principle in physics to other spheres of activity is boundless. In *Powers of Mind,*

Adam Smith suggests two examples: suppose an anthropologist travels to a mountaintop by helicopter to study a remote tribe. He may find that the tribespeople worship their old deities as they always have—or he may find himself part of their pantheon, a remarkable visitor from the heavens who arrived by magical means. Or imagine the television coverage of an election in a country as large as the United States. The polls close in the East, and news of one candidate's success is flashed to the West, where the polls won't close for two hours. Will this news prompt a rally on the part of the underdog's Western supporters, or will it convince them that their votes would be meaningless? Either way, the measurement of the phenomenon has changed the phenomenon. Another means of explaining the uncertainty principle is to say that it puts into the language of particle physics a homely precept, namely, that you can't do two things at once. Arthur Koestler attributes the static quality of certain Renaissance paintings to the fact that both foreground and background are in sharp focus, an optical impossibility because when we look at something closely its background becomes blurry and vice versa. The particle physicist finds himself in a similar quandary.

As these illustrations suggest, the problem is one of observation, as suggested by something called the paradox of Wigner's friend, after Nobel Prize winner Eugene Wigner. This paradox is founded on an earlier paradox, called the paradox of Schrödinger's cat (after Edwin Schrödinger, one of the original architects of QUANTUM MECHANICS), in which a cat in a box is killed by a mechanism triggered by a geiger counter that is tripped by an electron emitted from a radioactive substance after a certain predictable interval. Yet the cat is alive, according to the principles of quantum mechanics, until someone observes it in the state of death. If someone—Wigner's friend—opens the box and says that the cat is dead, is he to be believed? Wigner will have to observe his friend to make sure he is reporting accurately, but then someone will have to observe Wigner, *ad infinitum* until the entire population of the world is observing, with new observers being born every minute, each joining the phenomenon and becoming part of it. As the umpire says, "Some is balls and some is strikes, but until I calls 'em, they ain't nothin'."

Perhaps the most succinct summary of the uncertainty principle can be found in a poem by Reynolds Price called "The Annual Heron." The PERSONA of this poem takes a trout to a starving heron one winter but succeeds only in attracting dogs who attack the bird, prompting this observation: *"We tear what we touch."*

**unconscious**   The mental state characterized primarily by the functioning of the ID and the SUPEREGO; the state filled with repressed material that emerges in dreams, artistic creation, and inexplicable behavior rather than in ways sanctioned by the commonsensical EGO. Whereas the CONSCIOUS is clock-bound and is concerned with getting to work, shopping before the stores close, and so on, the unconscious is not. Describing the timelessness of the unconscious mental processes, Freud noted "that they are not ordered temporally, that time does not change them in any way and that the idea of time cannot be applied to them."

This difference notwithstanding, the interaction between conscious and unconscious is ceaseless and crucial. In *The Uses of Enchantment*, Bruno Bettelheim points out that a healthy child is constantly dealing with the repressed material of the unconscious, "not through rational comprehension of the nature and content of his unconscious, but by becoming familiar with it through spinning out daydreams—ruminating, rearranging, and fantasizing about suitable story elements in response to unconscious pressures. By doing this, the child fits unconscious content into conscious fantasies, which then enable him to deal with that content." Hence the importance of fairy tales, says Bettelheim. For example, a child who is disturbed by the occasional anger of an otherwise benevolent grandmother learns from "Little Red Riding Hood" that grandmothers are transformed from time to time, even though the benevolent old lady always returns at the end, following the destruction of her frightening alter ego, the wolf. The story helps the child to assign all negative character traits to the wolf and all positive ones to the grandmother, thus enabling the child to keep the image of the good grandmother separate, safe from unhealthy resentment. It is crucial not to explain these things to the child, says Bettelheim, because the child must struggle with the troublesome nature of life, neither being defeated by it nor fleeing from it. "Psychoanalysis itself is viewed as having the purpose of making life easy—but that is not what its founder intended. Psychoanalysis was created to enable man to accept the problematic nature of life without being defeated by it, or giving in to escapism. Freud's prescription is that only by struggling courageously against what seem like overwhelming odds can "man succeed in wringing meaning out of his existence." See COLLECTIVE UNCONSCIOUS and SUBCONSCIOUS.

**undistributed middle, fallacy of the**  See SYL-LOGISM.

**unified field theory**  Put simply by physicist Freeman Dyson, the unified field theory postulates a set of equations that would "account for everything that happens in nature . . . a unifying principle that would either explain everything or explain nothing." The intent is to unify the different fields that are used to describe nature—for example, to bring together the theories of relativity, which are mathematical descriptions of a vast universe, and the quantum theory, which describes a submicroscopic world. In both cases, what is being described is simply a relationship of bodies in a framework of space and time, attraction and repulsion, taking into account such matters as position, velocity, and mass.

Yet the two areas of inquiry are based on two completely different sets of physical laws. Some surface similarities between relativity theory and quantum theory suggest that the differences in their theoretical foundations may be eradicable, however, and Einstein's unified field theory—proposed in 1929, subsequently rejected, and reformulated in much more ambitious terms in 1949—attempted to do just that. Einstein's theory proposes a set of mutually consistent equations governing the workings of gravitation and electromagnetism. Still highly speculative, this theory promises to reconcile the macroscopic and microscopic universes; in Lincoln Barnett's words, "The whole complex of the universe will resolve into a homogeneous fabric in which matter and energy are indistinguishable and all forms of motion from the slow wheeling of the galaxies to the wild flight of electrons become simply changes in the structure and concentration of the primordial field."

**universe**   The totality of matter and energy both observed and postulated; to be strictly accurate, some scientists refer only to the "observable universe." See GALAXY.

# V

**vector**　See COMMUTATIVE MATHEMATICS.

**velleity**　The lowest form of desire; a wish so feeble that no effort is made to fulfill it.

Literature abounds with examples of velleities; thus in John Updike's novel *Rabbit Is Rich* a complacently married man thinks from time to time how pleasurable it would be to smash his wife's skull.

**vitalism**　A variety of beliefs, including the ENTELECHY and the ELAN VITAL, in a life force that is nonmaterial in nature. Vitalistic theories of the universe are opposed by theories of MECHANISM. See also TELEOLOGY.

**vorticism**　An early twentieth-century artistic movement represented by Gaudier-Brzeska in sculpture, Ezra Pound in poetry, and Wyndham Lewis in painting. William C. Wees says that vorticism in the visual arts is "a particular way of juxtaposing abstract, geometrical shapes" that was influential mainly in the years 1913–1915. But in poetry vorticism is often difficult to distinguish from IMAGISM, despite Pound's wish (in his memoir of Gaudier-Brzeska) for "a designation that would be equally applicable to a certain basis for all the arts. Obviously you cannot have 'cubist' poetry or 'imagist' painting." (In this connection, see also CUBISM.)

# W

**white dwarf**   See STELLAR EVOLUTION.


**wish-fulfillment**   A fantasy or dream that represents fulfillment of a CONSCIOUS or UNCONSCIOUS wish; also an act of the same nature. Freud wrote that "the repeating of what had been experienced in infancy is in itself the fulfillment of a wish."


**word-association test**   A type of PROJECTIVE TEST in which diagnostic conclusions are made on the basis of a subject's response to a list of specific words. Since the response is based on the subject's prior experience (real and imagined), the test is designed to reveal something about the subject's history, attitudes, and perceptions. C. G. Jung made the word-association test famous as a means of discovering COMPLEXES.

# Z

**Zeno's paradoxes**   Zeno of Elea propounded a number of paradoxes, the most famous of which says that a moving figure can never reach a given point because it must first cover half the distance to the point, then half the remaining distance, and so on, halving the distance each time and therefore never covering the total distance (as in a convergent infinite series; see under INFINITE SERIES). The point of the paradoxes is to show that common-sense ideas of motion and place are absurd.

Zeno was thought by Aristotle to be the first to use the dialectical method. In Zeno's case, this meant examining his opponent's propositions logically, by question and answer, until these propositions were reduced to paradoxical and contradictory statements. Zeno's method of argumentation is also known as REDUCTIO AD ABSURDUM.

**zero-sum game**   See GAME THEORY.

# GUIDE TO FURTHER STUDY

The book that is absolutely essential to one scholar is simply a dust-collector on the shelf of another. But I have found certain books indispensable in my interdisciplinary teaching and writing, and by describing my own priorities perhaps I can help others establish theirs.

On the desk closest to my typewriter, I always keep six books: the one-volume *New Columbia Encyclopedia*, *Webster's Third New International Dictionary*, *The Harper Dictionary of Modern Thought*, Peter Angeles's *Dictionary of Philosophy*, Siegfried Mandel's *Dictionary of Science*, and C. Hugh Holman's *Handbook to Literature*. These are books I consult almost every day.

On a nearby bookshelf are works that I consult somewhat less frequently. These include J. B. Priestley's *Literature and Western Man*, the eleven-volume *Story of Civilization* by Will and Ariel Durant, Michael H. Hart's *The 100: A Ranking of the Most Influential Persons in History*, the current volume of the *Information Please Almanac*, *Bartlett's Familiar Quotations*, and dictionaries in French, Spanish, German, Italian, and Latin.

On the same shelf as these secondary reference works are books by three authors to whom I can turn with certainty when I find myself in need of refreshment and instruction. They are Sigmund Freud and William and Henry James; as well as their writings, I keep at hand their biographies and a selection of the best critical studies on their work. Why these three? Because they wrote in the dawn of the present age. Had I lived in their day, no doubt I would have turned to Coleridge, Goethe, and Schopenhauer; had I lived in the middle of the nineteenth century, I would have begun with Voltaire, Rousseau, and Dr. Johnson. Freud and the two Jameses are not the only great minds writing at the beginning of our age, but they are the ones most congenial to me.

Among contemporaries I am partial to specialists rather than synthesizers. According to the myth, male and female were once one; then Zeus, seeing that they were arrogant, split them in two, and ever since they have been trying to reunite. This fundamental tension appeals to me not because of its metaphoric value but because it strikes me as realistic; the world is one and not-one at the same time. Besides, I have a fear of what Clifford Geertz calls "blurred genres" ("one waits only for quantum theory in verse or biography in algebra," says Geertz). Hence the usefulness to me of a second rank of authors after Freud and the Jameses: William Barrett, Jacques Barzun, Jeremy Bernstein, Bruno Bettelheim, Norman O. Brown, George P. Elliott, Arthur Koestler, Marvin Mudrick, Roger Shattuck, Lewis Thomas, and Edmund Wilson. I read these writers because each, though a specialist, is a broad and humane thinker; each is also unfailingly concrete in expression. I do not believe that all of their assertions are correct, but I do know from experience that these writers prompt me to make assertions of my own, and that too is why I read them.

These reference and primary sources (in addition to such newspapers and periodicals as *The New York Times* and its magazines, the *Times* of London and its educational and literary supplements, *The New Yorker*, *The New York Review of Books*, and *Science News*) are indispensable aids to interdisciplinary study. Beyond these printed materials, it would be impossible for me to overestimate the advantage of living within the widening circles of intellectual activity that constitute university life today. Within the last week, I have received a packet of material on computer-assisted literary research from a medical-school professor in Ohio, a letter on entropy from a childhood friend who now teaches sociology at Tulane University, and a paper on phenomenology from a secondary-school teacher in India. The other day a colleague walked in with an amusing anecdote about the discovery of noncommutative mathematics; a few hours later someone called in order to answer a question I had asked earlier about zero-sum games. These kinds of information are fortuitous and not available to everyone. I must put them under the category of extreme good luck; to the reader I can only say, go forth and find your own luck, and may it be as good as mine.

And of course to write a book like *The Plural World* takes all of the above sources of information and a small library besides. Each of the books and articles listed below has contributed in some important way to the overall enterprise. Those who want more information on a particular topic will be led to specific items in this list by references made within the text. Other readers will want to use the list as a general source of stimulating reading; neither group will go unrewarded.

Adcock, Craig. "The Transition from Dadaism to Surrealism."
Unpublished essay.

Angeles, Peter A. *Dictionary of Philosophy*. New York: Barnes
and Noble, 1981.

Appleton, Jay. *The Experience of Landscape*. London: Wiley,
1975.

Barnett, Lincoln. *The Universe and Dr. Einstein*. Rev. ed. New
York: Bantam, 1968; London: Collins, 1957.

Barrett, William. *The Illusion of Technique: A Search for Meaning in a Technological Civilization*. Garden City, N.Y.: Doubleday, 1978; London: Kimber, 1979.

—————. *Irrational Man: A Study in Existential Philosophy*.
Garden City, N.Y.: Doubleday, 1962; London: Greenwood,
1977.

—————. *Time of Need: Forms of Imagination in the Twentieth Century*. New York: Harper and Row, 1972.

Barth, John. "The Literature of Replenishment." *The Atlantic*,
245 (January 1980), 65-71.

Barzun, Jacques. *A Stroll with William James*. New York: Harper and Row, 1983.

Bazin, André. *What Is Cinema?* 2 vols. Berkeley, Los Angeles,
and London: University of California Press, 1967.

Beauvoir, Simone de. "Must We Burn Sade?" *The Marquis de
Sade*. Trans. Annette Michelson. New York: Grove, 1953.

Berne, Eric. *Games People Play: The Psychology of Human Relationships*. New York: Grove, 1977.

Bernstein, Jeremy. "A. I." *New Yorker*, December 14, 1981, 50ff.

—————. *A Comprehensible World: On Modern Science and
Its Origins*. New York: Random House, 1967.

—————. *Experiencing Science*. New York: Basic, 1978.

Bettelheim, Bruno. "Reflections: Freud and the Soul." *New
Yorker*, March 1, 1982, 52ff.

—————. *The Uses of Enchantment: The Meaning and Importance of Fairy Tales*. New York: Knopf, 1976; London:
Thames and Hudson, 1976.

Bly, Robert. "The Three Brains." *The New Naked Poetry*. Ed.
Stephen Berg and Robert Mezey. Indianapolis: Bobbs-Mer-
rill, 1976.

Bodkin, Maud. *Archetypal Patterns in Poetry: Psychological*

*Studies of Imagination.* London: Oxford University Press, 1965.

Breton, André. *Les Manifestes du Surréalisme.* Paris: Sagittaire, 1955.

Bright, James R., ed. *Technological Forecasting for Industry and Government: Methods and Applications.* Englewood Cliffs, N.J.: Prentice-Hall, 1968.

Brown, Norman O. *Life Against Death: The Psychoanalytical Meaning of History.* New York: Random House, 1959; London: Routledge and Kegan Paul, 1959.

Burke, Kenneth. *The Rhetoric of Religion: Studies in Logology.* Berkeley, Los Angeles, and London: University of California Press, 1970.

Burroughs, William. Interview in *Writers at Work*, 3rd series, ed. George Plimpton. New York; Viking, 1967; London: Secker and Warburg, 1968.

Burroway, Janet. *Writing Fiction: A Guide to Narrative Craft.* Boston: Little, Brown, 1982.

Butler, Christopher. *After the Wake: An Essay on the Contemporary Avant-Garde.* Oxford: Clarendon Press, 1969.

Calvino, Italo. *If on a Winter's Night a Traveler.* Trans. William Weaver. New York: Harcourt Brace Jovanovich, 1979; London: Secker and Warburg, 1981.

Campbell, Joseph. *The Masks of God: Creative Mythology.* 4 vols. New York: Viking, 1968; London: Secker and Warburg, 1968.

Cauvin, Jean Pierre. "Introduction: The Poethics of André Breton." *Poems of André Breton: A Bilingual Anthology.* Trans. and ed. Jean-Pierre Cauvin and Mary Ann Caws. Austin: University of Texas Press, 1983.

Cetron, Marvin J. *Technological Forecasting: A Practical Approach.* New York and London: Gordon and Breach, 1969.

Chénetier, Marc. Review of *La Condition Post-Moderne*, by Jean-François Lyotard. *American Book Review*, 5 (November-December 1982), 13.

Charbonnier, G. *Conversations with Claude Lévi-Strauss.* Trans. John and Doreen Weightman. London: Cape, 1969.

Church, Margaret. *Time and Reality: Studies in Contemporary Fiction.* Chapel Hill: University of North Carolina Press, 1963.

Cobb, Richard. *Death in Paris*. Oxford: Oxford University Press, 1978.

Connell, Evan S. "Otto and the Magi." *St. Augustine's Pigeon*. San Francisco: North Point, 1980.

Conway, Flo, and Jim Siegelman. *Snapping: America's Epidemic of Sudden Personality Change*. Philadelphia: Lippincott, 1978.

Cortázar, Julio. "The Southern Thruway." Trans. Suzanne Jill Levine. *Foreign Fictions*, ed. John Biguenet. New York: Random House, 1978.

Crane, Stephen. *Uncollected Writings*. Ed. Olov W. Fryckstedt. *Studia Anglistica Upsaliensia*, 1 (1963), 1-452.

Craven, Avery. *Reconstruction, the Ending of the Civil War*. New York and London: Holt, Rinehart and Winston, 1969.

Crews, Frederick. "Deconstructing a Discipline." *University Publishing*, no. 9 (Summer 1980), 2.

Crypton, Dr. (pseud.). "My Father's Son and Other Conundrums." *Science Digest*, 90 (January 1982), 106-108.

Culler, Jonathan. "Phenomenology and Structuralism," *Human Context*, 5 (1973), 35.

Damore, Leo. *In His Garden: The Anatomy of a Murderer*. New York: Arbor House, 1981.

Darwin, Charles. *On the Origin of Species by Means of Natural Selection*. Cambridge: Harvard University Press, 1964.

Davies, Robertson. *The Manticore*. Harmondsworth, England: Penguin, 1972.

Davis, Philip J., and Reuben Hersh. *The Mathematical Experience*. Boston: Birkhäuser, 1980; Brighton, England: Harvester, 1981.

Dekker, Eduard Douwes ("Multatuli"). *Max Havelaar*. Trans. Roy Edwards. Amherst: University of Massachusetts Press, 1981.

Di Piero, W. S. "Introduction" to *The Ellipse: Selected Poems of Leonard Sinisgalli*. Princeton: Princeton University Press, 1982.

Donoghue, Denis. "Her Deepest Passion Was D. H. Lawrence." *New York Times Book Review*, February 14, 1982, 3ff.

Dyson, Freeman. *Disturbing the Universe: A Life in Science*. New York and London: Harper and Row, 1979.

Edwards, Roy, and Ralph Pomeroy. "Working with Rothko."

*New American Review*, 12 (1971), 108-121.

Einstein, Albert. *Relativity: The Special and General Theory*. Trans. Robert W. Lawson. New York: Crown, 1961; London: Methuen, 1960.

Eliot, T. S. *Selected Prose of T. S. Eliot*. Ed. Frank Kermode. New York: Farrar, Straus and Giroux, 1975; London: Faber, 1975.

Elliott, George P. *Literature and the Modernist Deviation*. New York: Dutton, 1971.

*The Encyclopaedia Britannica*. 30 vols. 15th ed. Chicago: Encyclopaedia Britannica, 1979.

English, Horace B. *A Comprehensive Dictionary of Psychological and Psychoanalytical Terms*. New York: McKay, 1958; London: Longmans, Green, 1958.

Esslin, Martin. *The Theatre of the Absurd*. 3rd ed., rev. and enl. Harmondsworth, England: Penguin, 1980.

Evans, Christopher. *The Micro Millennium*. New York: Viking, 1980; first published as *The Mighty Micro*, London: Gollancz, 1979.

Fowler, Douglas. *A Reader's Guide to Gravity's Rainbow*. Ann Arbor: Ardis, 1980.

——————. *S. J. Perelman*. Boston: Twayne, 1983.

Fremont-Smith, Eliot. "Max & Rosie & and The Event Horizon." *Voice Literary Supplement (Village Voice)*, April 1982, 15.

Freud, Sigmund. *The Standard Edition of the Complete Psychological Works of Sigmund Freud*. Trans. from the German under the general editorship of James Strachey, in collaboration with Anna Freud, assisted by Alix Strachey and Alan Tyson. London: The Hogarth Press and the Institute of Psycho-Analysis, 1957.

*Funk & Wagnall's Standard College Dictionary*. New York: Harcourt, Brace and World, 1968.

Gardner, Martin. "Quantum Weirdness." *Discover*, October 1982, 69-75.

Geertz, Clifford. "Blurred Genres: The Refiguration of Social Thought." *American Scholar*, 49 (Spring 1980), 165-179.

Gellert, W., et al., eds. *The VNR Concise Encyclopedia of Mathematics*. New York and London: Van Nostrand Reinhold, 1977.

Gellner, Ernest. "The Paradox in Paradigms." *Times Literary Supplement*, April 23, 1982, 451-452.

Gilligan, Carol. *In a Different Voice: Psychological Theory and Women's Development*. Cambridge: Harvard University Press, 1982.

Hagen, Richard. *The Bio-Sexual Factor*. Garden City N.Y.: Doubleday 1979.

Hallie, Philip P. *The Paradox of Cruelty*. Middletown, Conn.: Wesleyan University Press, 1969.

Hardy, G. H. *A Mathematician's Apology*. Cambridge: Cambridge University Press, 1967.

Harris, Sydney J. "Faculties Are Hung Up on Protecting Turf." *Tallahassee Democrat*, April 15, 1983, 5A.

Hart, Michael H. *The 100: A Ranking of the Most Influential Persons in History*. New York: Hart, 1978.

Hemingway, Ernest. *A Moveable Feast*. New York: Scribner, 1964; London; Cape, 1964.

Herrigel, Eugen. *Zen in the Art of Archery*. Trans. R. F. C. Hull. New York: Pantheon, 1953; London: Routledge and Kegan Paul, 1953.

Hilts, Philip. "Odd Man Out." *Omni*, 3 (January 1981), 68ff.

Himmelfarb, Gertrude. "A History of the New History." *New York Times Book Review*, January 10, 1982, 9.

Hofstadter, Douglas R. *Gödel, Escher, Bach: An Eternal Golden Braid*. New York: Random House, 1980; Harmondsworth, England: Penguin, 1981.

Hough, Graham. "Just a Soupçon of Paris." *Times Literary Supplement*, June 26, 1981, 725.

Ionesco, Eugène. "Rhinoceros." Trans. Jean Stewart. *Foreign Fictions*, ed. John Biguenet. New York: Random House, 1978.

James, Glenn and Robert C. *Mathematics Dictionary*. 4th ed. New York and London: Van Nostrand Reinhold, 1976.

James, William. *The Principles of Psychology*. 2 vols. New York and London: Macmillan, 1980.

Jastrow, Robert. *God and the Astronomers*. New York: Norton, 1978.

Jaynes, Julian. *The Origin of Consciousness in the Breakdown of the Bicameral Mind*. Boston: Houghton Mifflin, 1976.

Stapp, H. P. "Bell's Theorem and World Process." *Nuovo*

Jonas, Gerald. "Douglas Hofstadter." *New York Times Book Review*, December 28, 1980, 18.

Jones, Ernest. *The Life and Work of Sigmund Freud.* Ed. and abridged Lionel Trilling and Steven Marcus. New York: Basic Books, 1961; Harmondsworth, England: Penguin, 1964.

Josipovici, Gabriel. "Möbius the Stripper: A Topological Exercise." *Writing Fiction: A Guide to Narrative Craft*, by Janet Burroway. Boston: Little, Brown, 1982.

Joyce, James. *Finnegans Wake.* New York: Viking, 1939; London: Faber, 1939.

Jung, C. G. *Memories, Dreams, Reflections.* Recorded and ed. Aniela Jaffé. Trans. Richard and Clara Winston. New York: Random House, 1965.

Kasner, Edward, and James Newman. *Mathematics and the Imagination.* New York: Simon and Schuster, 1940; London: Bell, 1949.

Kaufmann, William J., III. *Black Holes and Warped Spacetime.* San Francisco: Freeman, 1979.

Kendrick, Walter. "Deep in the Heart of Texts." *Voice Literary Supplement (Village Voice)*, November 1981, 12.

Kennedy, William. *Billy Phelan's Greatest Game.* New York and Harmondsworth, England: Penguin, 1983.

Kinnell, Galway. "Dear Stranger Extant in Memory by the Blue Juniata." *The Book of Nightmares.* Boston: Houghton Mifflin, 1971.

Kirby, David. *The Sun Rises in the Evening: Monism and Quietism in Western Culture.* Metuchen, N.J., and London: Scarecrow, 1982.

Kline, Morris. *Mathematics: The Loss of Certainty.* New York: Oxford University Press, 1980.

Koestler, Arthur. *The Ghost in the Machine.* New York: Macmillan, 1967; London: Hutchinson, 1967.

————. *The Roots of Coincidence.* London: Hutchinson, 1972.

Kolb, Harold H., Jr. "In Search of Definition: American Literary Realism and the Clichés." *American Literary Realism*, 2 (Summer 1969), 165-173.

Kuhn, Thomas S. *The Structures of Scientific Revolutions.*

Chicago and London: University of Chicago Press, 1962.

Kunitz, Stanley. "A Kind of Order." *A Kind of Order*. Boston: Little, Brown, 1975.

Langbaum, Robert. "Current Trends in Literary Criticism." *National Forum*, 60 (Fall 1980), 20-22.

Leitch, Vincent B. "The Book of Deconstructive Criticism." *Studies in the Literary Imagination*, 12 (Spring 1979), 19-39.

Lekachman, Robert. In "Critics' Christmas Choices." *Commonweal*, December 4, 1981, 700-701.

Lesser, Wendy. "Fiction and Reality." *Threepenny Review*, 2 (Winter 1982), 3.

Lévi-Strauss, Claude. *Anthropologie Structurale*. 2 vols. Paris: Plon, 1958.

Levy, Steven. "Hackers in Paradise: A Beautiful Obsession with the Binary World." *Rolling Stone*, April 15, 1982, 42-51.

Lewis, C. S. *The Problem of Pain*. New York: Macmillan, 1962.

Lhamon, W. T. "Lee Strasberg: The Man Who Turned Acting Inside Out." *Florida Flambeau*, February 23, 1982, 9.

Lorenz, Konrad. *King Solomon's Ring*. London: Methuen, 1964.

Lucas, F. L. *The Decline and Fall of the Romantic Ideal*. Cambridge: Cambridge University Press, 1963.

Lunde, Donald T., and Jefferson Morgan. *The Die Song: A Journey into the Mind of a Mass Murderer*. New York: Norton, 1970.

Lyotard, Jean-François. *La Condition Post-Moderne*. Paris: Editions de Minuit, 1979.

McCarthy, Mary. "Settling the Colonel's Hash." *On the Contrary*. New York: Noonday, 1962; London: Heinemann, 1962.

—————. *The Stones of Florence and Venice Observed*. Harmondsworth, England: Penguin, 1972.

Mailloux, Steven. *Interpretive Conventions: The Reader in the Study of American Fiction*. Ithaca and London: Cornell University Press, 1982.

Malcolm, Janet. "The Impossible Profession—I." *New Yorker*, November 24, 1980, 55ff.

Mandel, Siegfried. *Dictionary of Science*. New York: Dell, 1969.

Martin, Jay. *Harvests of Change: American Literature 1865–1914*. Englewood Cliffs, N.J.: Prentice-Hall, 1967.

Martino, Joseph P. *Technological Forecasting for Decisionmak-*

*ing.* New York: American Elsevier, 1972.

Marx, Karl. *Essential Writings.* Ed. David Caute. New York: Crown, 1970.

Molinos, Michael de. *The Spiritual Guide Which Disentangles the Soul.* Ed. Kathleen Lyttelton. London: Methuen, 1950.

Morris, Richard. *The Fate of the Universe.* New York: Playboy, 1982.

Myers, David, and Thomas Ludwig. "Let's Cut the Poortalk." *Saturday Review,* October 28, 1978, 24-25.

Nalley, Richard, et al. "Sociobiology: A New View of Human Nature." *Science Digest,* 90 (July 1982), 62-69.

Nuttall, John. "Theoreticians Consider Three-Body Collision Problem." *Physics Today,* 21 (July 1968), 107-109.

O'Brien, Tim. *Going After Cacciato.* New York: Dell, 1975.

O'Connor, Johnson. *Science Vocabulary Builder.* Boston: Human Engineering Laboratory, 1956.

Peierls, Rudolf. "Odd Couple." *New York Review of Books,* February 18, 1982, 16-18.

Perrault, John. "Robots in Love." *Village Voice,* October 5, 1982, 24.

Plendl, Hans. "The Heisenberg Uncertainty Principle: Ambiguity and Precision in the Description of Nature." Unpublished essay.

_____ . "Mirrors and Our Understanding of Nature." Unpublished essay.

_____ . "The World According to Quarks." Unpublished essay.

Pound, Ezra. *Gaudier-Brzeska: A Memoir.* New York: New Directions, 1970; London: Laidlaw and Laidlaw, 1939.

Price, Reynolds. "The Annual Heron." *Vital Provisions.* New York: Atheneum, 1982.

Reese, William L. *Dictionary of Philosophy and Religion: Eastern and Western Thought.* Atlantic Highlands, N.J.: Humanities, 1980; Hassocks, England: Harvester, 1980.

Riencourt, Amaury de. *The Eye of Shiva: Eastern Mysticism and Science.* New York: Morrow, 1981.

Ritvo, Harriet. "Darkness Visible." *Threepenny Review,* 3 (Summer 1982), 8-9.

Roszak, Theodore. "In Search of the Miraculous." *Harper's*, 262 (January 1981), 54-62.

——————. *The Making of a Counter Culture: Reflections on the Technocratic Society and Its Youthful Opposition*. Garden City, N.Y.: Doubleday, 1969; London: Faber, 1970.

Roth, Philip. *The Professor of Desire*. New York: Farrar, Straus and Giroux, 1977; London: Cape, 1978

Russell, Bertrand. *A History of Western Philosophy*. New York: Simon and Schuster, 1945; London: Allen and Unwin, 1948.

Sade, Marquis de. "Dialogue Between a Priest and a Dying Man (1782)." *New Humanist*, 97 (Summer 1982), 15-18.

Saltman, Paul. "Humanists and Scientists Must Try to Give Us a New Mythology." *Chronicle of Higher Education*, December 8, 1982, 64.

Schwarz, Ted. *The Hillside Strangler: A Murderer's Mind*. New York: Doubleday, 1981.

Searle, John R. "The Myth of the Computer." *New York Review of Books*, April 29, 1982, 3-6.

Seymour-Smith, Martin. *Robert Graves: His Life and Work*. New York: Holt, Rinehart and Winston, 1982; London: Hutchinson, 1982.

Shapiro, David, ed. *Social Realism: Art as a Weapon*. New York: Ungar, 1973.

Shattuck, Roger. *The Banquet Years: The Origins of the Avant-Garde in France, 1885 to World War I*. Rev. ed. New York: Random House, 1968; London: Cape, 1969.

Smith, Adam. *Powers of Mind*. New York: Ballantine, 1975; London: W.H. Allen, 1976.

——————. *Supermoney*. New York: Random House, 1972; London: Joseph, 1973.

Snow, C. P. *The Two Cultures: And a Second Look*. New York: New American Library, 1963; Cambridge: Cambridge University Press, 1964.

Sorrentino, Gilbert. *Aberration of Starlight*. New York: Random House, 1980; London: Boyars, 1981.

Stanley, Steven. "The New Evolution." *Johns Hopkins Magazine*, 33 (June 1982), 6-11.

*Cimento,* 29 (October 11, 1975), 270-276.

——————. "S-Matrix Interpretation of Quantum Theory." *Physical Review,* D3, 1971, 1303ff; quoted in Zukav.

Stokes, Geoffrey. "The Paranoid Style in Yankee Baseball." *Village Voice,* April 19, 1983, 11.

Tanner, Tony. "Notes for a Comparison Between American and European Romanticism." *Journal of American Studies,* 2 (1968), 83-103.

Taylor, Gordon Rattray. *The Natural History of the Mind.* New York: Dutton, 1979; London: Secker and Warburg, 1979.

Taylor, John Russell. "Tragi-comic Mystery of the Twentieth Century." *Times* (London), August 10, 1982, 7.

Tomkins, Calvin. "The Art World: What the Hand Knows." *New Yorker,* May 2, 1983, 113ff.

——————. *Off the Wall: Robert Rauschenburg and the Art World of Our Time.* New York: Penguin, 1981.

Trilling, Diana. *Mrs. Harris: The Death of the Scarsdale Diet Doctor.* New York: Harcourt Brace Jovanovich, 1981.

Turner, Frederick Jackson. *The Frontier in American History.* New York: Holt, Rinehart and Winston, 1962.

Tzara, Tristan. *Seven Dada Manifestos and Lampisteries.* Trans. Barbara Wright. London: Calder, 1977.

Von Neumann, John, and Oskar Morganstern. *Theory of Games and Economic Behavior.* 3rd ed. Princeton: Princeton University Press, 1953; London: Oxford University Press, 1953.

Wade, David. "God versus Darwin." *Times* (London), August 7, 1982, 6.

Walker, David. " 'Structuralism' Debate Moves to English Dept. at Oxford." *Chronicle of Higher Education,* December 15, 1982, 26.

Watson, James D. *The Double Helix: Being a Personal Account of the Structure of DNA.* New York: Atheneum, 1968; London: Weidenfeld and Nicolson, 1968.

Weaver, Warren. *Lady Luck: The Theory of Probability.* New York: Anchor, 1963.

*Webster's Third New International Dictionary, Unabridged.* Springfield, Mass.: Merriam, 1981.

Wees, William C. *Vorticism and the English Avant-Garde.* Toronto: University of Toronto Press, 1972; Manchester:

Manchester University Press, 1972.

Weil, Andrew. *The Natural Mind: A New Way of Looking at Drugs and the Higher Consciousness.* Boston: Houghton Mifflin, 1972.

Weschler, Lawrence. "Profiles: Taking Art of Point Zero—I." *New Yorker*, March 8, 1982, 48-95.

West, Susan. "Fighting Lamarck's Shadow." *Science News*, March 14, 1981, 174-175.

Wharton, Edith. *A Backward Glance.* New York and London: Appleton Century, 1934.

Wiener, Norbert. *Cybernetics.* 2nd ed. New York and London: Wiley, 1961.

Wilson, Edmund. *Axel's Castle: A Study in the Imaginative Literature of 1870–1930.* New York and London: Scribner, 1931.

Wilson, Edward O. *Sociobiology: The New Synthesis.* Cambridge: Harvard University Press, 1975.

Wilson, Robert A. "Mere Coincidence?" *Science Digest*, 90 (January 1982), 82ff.

Wimsatt, W. K., Jr., and Monroe C. Beardsley. "The Affective Fallacy." *The Verbal Icon: Studies in the Meaning of Poetry.* Lexington: University of Kentucky Press, 1954.

Wolman, Benjamin B., et al., comps. and eds. *Dictionary of Behavioral Science.* New York and London: Van Nostrand Reinhold, 1973.

Woodward, C. Vann. "A Short History of American History." *New York Times Book Review*, August 8, 1982, 3ff.

Woodward, Kenneth, et al. "A New Look at Lit Crit." *Newsweek*, June 22, 1981, 80-83.

Zipes, Jack D. *The Great Refusal: Studies of the Romantic Hero in German and American Literature.* Bad Homburg: Athenäum Verlag, 1970.